5 Practices

for Orchestrating Productive Mathematics Discussions

Includes Professional Development Guide

Margaret S. Smith
University of Pittsburgh
Pittsburgh, Pennsylvania

Mary Kay Stein
University of Pittsburgh
Pittsburgh, Pennsylvania

NATIONAL COUNCIL OF
TEACHERS OF MATHEMATICS

CORWIN
A SAGE Company

Copyright © 2011 by
THE NATIONAL COUNCIL OF TEACHERS OF MATHEMATICS, INC.
1906 Association Drive, Reston, VA 20191-1502
(703) 620-9840; (800) 235-7566; www.nctm.org
All rights reserved
Fourteenth printing 2016

Library of Congress Cataloging-in-Publication Data

Smith, Margaret Schwan.
  5 practices for orchestrating productive mathematics discussions /
Margaret S. Smith, Mary Kay Stein.
    p. cm.
  Includes bibliographical references.
  ISBN 978-0-87353-677-6
  1. Communication in mathematics. 2. Mathematics--Study and teaching
(Primary) 3. Mathematics--Study and teaching (Secondary) I. Stein,
Mary Kay. II. Title. III. Title: Five practices for orchestrating
productive mathematics discussions.
  QA41.4.S65 2011
  510.71--dc22

                                                          2011007321

The National Council of Teachers of Mathematics is the public voice of mathematics education, supporting teachers to ensure equitable mathematics learning of the highest quality for all students through vision, leadership, professional development, and research.

Printed in the United States of America

Contents

Preface

In this book, we present and discuss a framework for orchestrating mathematically productive discussions that are rooted in student thinking. The framework identifies a set of instructional practices that will help teachers achieve high-demand learning objectives by using student work as the launching point for discussions in which important mathematical ideas are brought to the surface, contradictions are exposed, and understandings are developed or consolidated. The premise underlying the book is that the identification and use of a codified set of practices can make student-centered approaches to mathematics instruction accessible to and manageable for more teachers. By giving teachers a road map of things that they can do in advance and during whole-class discussions, these practices have the potential for helping teachers to more effectively orchestrate discussions that are responsive to both students and the discipline.

Throughout the book, we illustrate the practices in real classrooms with which we have become acquainted through research or professional practice (e.g., through teachers with whom we have worked in professional development initiatives). In particular, we make significant use of two classroom lessons: the Case of Darcy Dunn and the Case of Nick Bannister. The Case of Darcy Dunn is introduced in chapter 3 as a vehicle for investigating the five practices in action, and it is revisited in subsequent chapters as the practices are explored more fully. The Case of Nick Bannister is explored in considerable depth in chapters 4 and 5 as each of the five practices is examined in detail, and then it is referred to again in subsequent chapters as broader issues are considered.

Following research that has established the importance of learners' construction of their own knowledge (Bransford, Brown, and Cocking 2000), we have designed this book to encourage the active engagement of readers. In several places, we have provided notes (titled "Active Engagement") that suggest ways in which the reader can engage with specific artifacts of classroom practice (e.g., narrative cases of classroom instruction, transcripts of classroom interactions, instructional tasks, samples of student work). Rather than passively read the book from cover to cover, readers are encouraged to take our suggestions to heart and pause for a moment to grapple with the information in the ways suggested. By actively processing the information, readers' understandings will be deepened, as will their ability to access and use the knowledge flexibly in their own professional life. In addition, at the end of chapters 4, 5, 6, and 7, we have provided suggestions (titled "Try This!") regarding how a teacher can explore the ideas from the chapter in their own classrooms.

Although the primary focus of the book is the five practices model (chapters 1, 3, 4, and 5), it also explores other issues that support teachers' ability to orchestrate productive classroom discussions. Specifically, chapter 2 emphasizes the need to set clear goals for what students will learn as a result of instruction and to identify a mathematical task that is consistent with those learning goals prior to engaging in the five practices. Chapter 6 focuses explicitly on the types of questions that teachers can ask to challenge students' thinking and the moves that teachers can make to promote the participation of students in whole-class discussions. Chapter 7 situates the five practices model for facilitating a discussion within the broader context of preparing for a lesson and introduces a tool for comprehensive lesson planning in which the five practices are embedded. The book concludes with chapter 8, which discusses ways in which teachers can work with colleagues, coaches, and school leaders to ensure that they have the time, materials, and access to expertise that they need to learn to orchestrate productive discussions.

Introduction

As we move into the second decade of the twenty-first century, one thing is clear: Our country needs highly trained workers who can wrestle with complex problems. Gone are the days when basic skills could be counted on to yield high-paying jobs and an acceptable standard of living. Especially needed are individuals who can think, reason, and engage effectively in quantitative problem solving.

The instructional practices used in the majority of our nation's classrooms will not prepare students for these new demands. National studies have shown that American students are not routinely asked to engage in conceptual thinking or complex problem solving (Stigler and Hiebert 1999). Most schoolwork consists of assignments composed of "problems" for which students have been taught a preferred method of solving. There is little engagement of student "thinking" in such tasks, only the straightforward application of previously learned skills and recall of memorized facts. It is unrealistic to expect students to learn to grapple with the unstructured, messy challenges of today's world if they are forced to sit silently in rows, complete basic skills worksheets, and engage in teacher-led "discussions" that consist of literal, fact-based questions and answers.

What kind of learning experiences *will* prepare students for the demands of the twenty-first century? *Research tells us that complex knowledge and skills are learned through social interaction* (Vygotsky 1978; Lave and Wenger 1991). We learn through a process of knowledge construction that requires us to actively manipulate and refine information and then integrate it with our prior understandings. Social interaction provides us with the opportunity to use others as resources, to share our ideas with others, and to participate in the joint construction of knowledge. In mathematics classrooms, high-quality discussions support student learning of mathematics by helping students learn how to communicate their ideas, making students' thinking public so it can be guided in mathematically sound directions, and encouraging students to evaluate their own and each other's mathematical ideas. These are all important features of what it means to be "mathematically literate."

Creating discussion-based opportunities for student learning will require learning on the part of many teachers. First, teachers will need to learn how to select and set up cognitively challenging instructional tasks in their classrooms, since such high-level tasks provide the grist for worthwhile discussions. Over the years, however, most textbooks have fed teachers a steady diet of routine, procedural tasks around which it would be difficult, if not impossible, to organize an engaging discussion.

Second, teachers must learn how to support their students as they engage with and discuss their solutions to cognitively challenging tasks. We know from our own past research that once high-level tasks are introduced in the classroom, many teachers have difficulty maintaining the cognitive demand of those tasks as students engage with them (Stein, Grover, and Henningsen 1996). Students often end up thinking and reasoning at a lower level than the task is intended to elicit. One of the reasons for this is teachers' difficulties in orchestrating discussions that productively use students' ideas and strategies that are generated in response to high-level tasks.

A typical lesson that uses a high-level instructional task proceeds in three phases. It begins with the teacher's launching of a mathematical problem that embodies important mathematical ideas and can be solved in multiple ways. During this "launch phase," the teacher introduces students to the problem, the tools that are available for working on it, and the nature of the products that the students will be expected to produce. This phase is followed by the "explore phase," in which students work on the problem, often discussing it in pairs or small groups. As students work on the problem, they are encouraged to solve it in whatever way makes sense to them and be prepared to explain their approach to others in the class. The lesson then concludes with a whole-class discussion and summary of various student-generated approaches to solving the problem. During this "discuss and summarize" phase, a variety of approaches to the problem are displayed for the whole class to view and discuss.

Why are these end-of-class discussions so difficult to orchestrate? Research tells us that students learn when they are encouraged to become the authors of their own ideas and when they are held accountable for reasoning about and understanding key ideas (Engle and Conant 2002). In practice, doing both of these simultaneously is very difficult. By their nature, high-level tasks do not lead all students to solve the problem in the same way. Rather, teachers can and should expect to see varied (both correct and incorrect) approaches to solving the task during the discussion phase of the lesson. In theory, this is a good thing because students are "authoring" (or constructing) their own ways of solving the problem.

The challenge rests in the fact that teachers must also align the many disparate approaches that students generate in response to high-level tasks with the learning goal of the lesson. It is the teachers' responsibility to move students collectively toward, and hold them accountable for, the development of a set of ideas and processes that are central to the discipline—those that are widely accepted as worthwhile and important in mathematics as well as necessary for students' future learning of mathematics in school. If the teacher fails to do this, the balance tips too far toward student authority, and classroom discussions become unmoored from accepted disciplinary understandings.

The key is to maintain the right balance. Too much focus on accountability can undermine students' authority and sense making and, unwittingly, encourage increased reliance on teacher direction. Students quickly get the message—often from subtle cues—that "knowing mathematics" means using only those strategies that have been validated by the teacher or textbook; correspondingly, they learn not to use or trust their own reasoning. Too much focus on student authorship, on the other hand, leads to classroom discussions that are free-for-alls.

Successful or Superficial? Discussion in David Crane's Classroom

In short, the teacher's role in discussions is critical. Without expert guidance, discussions in mathematics classrooms can easily devolve into the teacher taking over the lesson and providing a "lecture," on the one hand, or, on the other, the students presenting an unconnected series of show-and-tell demonstrations, all of which are treated equally and together illuminate little about the mathematical ideas that are the goal of the lesson. Consider, for example, the following vignette (from Stein and colleagues [2008]), featuring a fourth-grade teacher, David Crane.

ACTIVE ENGAGEMENT 0.1
As you read the Case of David Crane, identify instances of student authorship of ideas and approaches, as well as instances of holding students accountable to the discipline.

Leaves and Caterpillars: The Case of David Crane

Students in Mr. Crane's fourth-grade class were solving the following problem: "A fourth-grade class needs 5 leaves each day to feed its 2 caterpillars. How many leaves would the students need each day for 12 caterpillars?" Mr. Crane told his students that they could solve the problem any way they wanted, but he emphasized that they needed to be able to explain how they got their answer and why it worked.

As students worked in pairs to solve the problem, Mr. Crane walked around the room, making sure that students were on task and making progress on the problem. He was pleased to see that students were using many different approaches to the problem—making tables, drawing pictures, and, in some cases, writing explanations.

He noticed that two pairs of students had gotten wrong answers (see fig. 0.1). Mr. Crane wasn't too concerned about the incorrect responses, however, since he felt that once several correct solution strategies were presented, these students would see what they did wrong and have new strategies for solving similar problems in the future.

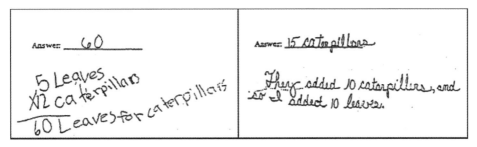

Fig. 0.1. Solutions produced by Darnell and Marcus (left) and Missy and Kate (right)

When most students were finished, Mr. Crane called the class together to discuss the problem. He began the discussion by asking for volunteers to share their solutions and strategies, being careful to avoid calling on the students with incorrect solutions. Over the course of the next 15 minutes, first Kyra, then Jason, Jamal, Melissa, Martin, and Janine volunteered to present the solutions to the task that they and their partners had created (see fig. 0.2). During each presentation, Mr. Crane made sure to ask each presenter questions that helped the student to clarify and justify the work. He concluded the class by telling students that the problem could be solved in many different ways and now, when they solved a problem like this, they could pick the way they liked best because all the ways gave the same answer.

Janine's Work	Kyra's Work
Answer: 30 \\\ \\\\\\\\\\ if each of these caterpillars need 2½ leaves a day then you just X's 2½ x's 12 = 30.	Answer: 30 2½ 2½ 2½ 2½ 2½ 2½ 2½ 2½ 2½ 2½ 2½ 2½

Jamal's Work	Martin's Work
Answer: 30 leaves leaves: 5 | 10 | 15 | 20 | 25 | 30 caterpillars: 2 | 4 | 6 | 8 | 10 | 12	Answer: 30 leaves

Jason's Work	Melissa's Work
Answer: 30 If it takes 5 leafs for two caterpillars, you just count by twos, until you come to half of 12. The number is six, and then you multiply 5×6, and it equals 30.	Answer: 30

# of caterpillars	# of leaves
2	5
2	5
2	5
2	5
2	5
+2	+5
12	30

Fig. 0.2. Solutions shared by students in Mr. Crane's class

Analyzing the Case of David Crane

Some would consider Mr. Crane's lesson exemplary. Indeed, Mr. Crane did many things well, including allowing students to construct their own way of solving this cognitively challenging task and stressing the importance of students' being able to explain their reasoning. Students were working with partners and publicly sharing their solutions and strategies with their peers; their ideas appeared to be respected. All in all, students in Mr. Crane's class had the opportunity to become the "authors" of their own knowledge of mathematics.

However, a more critical eye might have noted that the string of presentations did not build toward important mathematical ideas. The upshot of the discussion appeared to be "the more ways of solving the problem, the better," but, in fact, Mr. Crane held each student accountable for knowing only one way to solve the problem. In addition, although Mr. Crane observed students as they worked, he did not appear to use this time to assess what students understood about proportional reasoning or to select particular students' work to feature in the whole-class discussion. Furthermore, he gathered no information regarding whether the two pairs of students who had gotten the wrong answer (Darnell and Marcus, and Missy and Kate) were helped by the student presentations of correct strategies. Had they diagnosed the faulty reasoning in their approaches?

In fact, we argue that much of the discussion in Mr. Crane's classroom was show-and-tell, in which students with correct answers each take turns sharing their solution strategies. The teacher did little filtering of the mathematical ideas that each strategy helped to illustrate, nor did he make any attempt to highlight those ideas. In addition, the teacher did not draw connections among different solution methods or tie them to important disciplinary methods or mathematical ideas. Finally, he gave no attention to weighing which strategies might be most useful, efficient, accurate, and so on, in particular circumstances. All were treated as equally good.

In short, providing students with cognitively demanding tasks with which to engage and then conducting show-and-tell discussions cannot be counted on to move an entire class forward mathematically. Indeed, this kind of practice has been criticized for creating classroom environments in which nearly complete control of the mathematical agenda is relinquished to students. Some teachers misperceived the appeal to honor students' thinking and reasoning as a call for a complete moratorium on teachers' shaping of the quality of students' mathematical thinking. As a result of the lack of guidance with respect to what teachers *could* do to encourage rigorous mathematical thinking and reasoning, many teachers were left feeling that they should avoid telling students anything.

A related criticism of inquiry-oriented lessons concerns the fragmented and often incoherent nature of the discuss-and-summarize phases of lessons. In these show-and-tells, as exemplified in David Crane's classroom, one student presentation would follow another with limited teacher (or student) commentary and no assistance with respect to drawing connections among the methods or tying them to widely shared disciplinary methods and concepts. The discussion offered no mathematical or other reason for students to necessarily listen to or try to understand the methods of their classmates. As illustrated in Mr. Crane's comment at the end of the class, students could simply "pick the way they liked best." This type of situation has led to an increasingly recognized dilemma associated with inquiry- and discovery-based approaches to teaching: the challenge of aligning students' developing ideas and methods with the disciplinary ideas that they ultimately are accountable for knowing.

In sum, David Crane did little to encourage accountability to the discipline of mathematics. How could he have more firmly supported student accountability without undermining student authority? The single most important thing that he could have done would be to have set a clear goal for what he wanted students to learn from the lesson. Without a learning objective in mind, the various solutions that were presented, although all correct, were scattered in the "mathematical landscape." If, however, he had targeted the learning goal of, for example, making sure that all students recognized that the relationship between caterpillars and leaves was multiplicative and not additive, he might have monitored students' work with this in mind. Whose work illustrated the multiplicative relationship particularly well? Did the students' work include examples of different ways of illustrating this relationship—examples that could connect with known mathematical strategies (e.g., unit rate, scaling up)? This assessment of student work would have allowed him to be more deliberate about which students he selected to present during the discussion phase. He might even have wanted to have the incorrect, additive solutions displayed so that students could recognize the faulty reasoning that underlie them. With an array of purposefully selected strategies presented, Mr. Crane would then be in a position to steer the discussion toward a more mathematically satisfying conclusion.

Conclusion

The Case of David Crane illustrates the need for guidance in shaping classroom discussions and maximizing their potential to extend students' thinking and connect it to important mathematical ideas. The chapters that follow offer this guidance by elaborating a practical framework, based on five doable instructional practices, for orchestrating and managing productive classroom discussions.

Introducing the Five Practices

Many teachers are daunted by an approach to pedagogy that builds on student thinking. Some are worried about content coverage, asking, "How can I be assured that students will learn what I am responsible for teaching if I don't march through the material and tell them everything they need to know?" Others—teachers who perhaps are already convinced of the importance of student thinking—may be nonetheless worried about their ability to diagnose students' thinking on the fly and to quickly devise responses that will guide students to the correct mathematical understanding.

Teachers are correct when they acknowledge that this type of teaching is demanding. It requires knowledge of the relevant mathematical content, of student thinking about that content, and of the subtle pedagogical "moves" that a teacher can make to lead discussions in fruitful directions, along with the ability to rapidly apply all of this in specific circumstances. Yet, we have seen many teachers learn to teach in this way, with the help of the five practices.

We think of the five practices as skillful improvisation. The practices that we have identified are meant to make student-centered instruction more manageable by moderating the degree of improvisation required by the teacher during a discussion. Instead of focusing on in-the-moment responses to student contributions, the practices emphasize the importance of planning. Through planning, teachers can anticipate likely student contributions, prepare responses that they might make to them, and make decisions about how to structure students' presentations to further their mathematical agenda for the lesson. We turn now to an explication of the five practices.

The Five Practices

The five practices were designed to help teachers to use students' responses to advance the mathematical understanding of the class as a whole by providing teachers with some control over what is likely to happen in the discussion as well as more time to make instructional decisions by shifting some of the decision making to the planning phase of the lesson. The five practices are—

1. ***anticipating*** likely student responses to challenging mathematical tasks;

2. ***monitoring*** students' actual responses to the tasks (while students work on the tasks in pairs or small groups);

3. ***selecting*** particular students to present their mathematical work during the whole-class discussion;

4. ***sequencing*** the student responses that will be displayed in a specific order; and

5. ***connecting*** different students' responses and connecting the responses to key mathematical ideas.

Each practice is described in more detail in the following sections, which illustrate them by identifying what Mr. Crane *could have done* in the Leaves and Caterpillars lesson (presented in the introduction), to move student thinking more skillfully toward the goal of recognizing that the relationship between caterpillars and leaves is multiplicative, not additive.

Anticipating

The first practice is to make an effort to actively envision how students might mathematically approach the instructional task or tasks that they will work on. This involves much more than simply evaluating whether a task is at the right level of difficulty or of sufficient interest to students, and it goes beyond considering whether or not they are getting the "right" answer.

Anticipating students' responses involves developing considered expectations about how students might mathematically interpret a problem, the array of strategies—both correct and incorrect—that they might use to tackle it, and how those strategies and interpretations might relate to the mathematical concepts, representations, procedures, and practices that the teacher would like his or her students to learn.

Anticipating requires that teachers do the problem as many ways as they can. Sometimes teachers find that it is helpful to expand on what they might be able to think of individually by working on the task with colleagues, reviewing responses to the task that might be available (e.g., work produced by students in the previous year, responses that are published along with tasks in supplementary materials), and consulting research on student learning of the mathematical ideas embedded in the task. For example, research suggests that students often use additive strategies (such Missy and Kate's response, shown in fig. 0.1) to solve tasks like the Leaves and Caterpillars problem, in which there is a multiplicative relationship between quantities (Hart 1981; Heller et al. 1989; Kaput and West 1994). Anticipating this approach in advance of the lesson would have made it possible for Mr. Crane to recognize it when his students produced it and carefully consider what actions he might take should they do so (e.g., what questions to ask so that students become aware of the multiplicative nature of the relationship between the caterpillars and leaves, how to bring up the solution during discussion so that all students might consider why it is not a valid method).

In addition, if Mr. Crane had solved the problem ahead of time in as many ways as possible, he might have realized that there were at least two different strategies for arriving at the correct answer—unit rate and scale factor—and that each of these could be expressed with different representations (pictures, tables, and written explanations).

Monitoring

Monitoring student responses involves paying close attention to students' mathematical thinking and solution strategies as they work on the task. Teachers generally do this by circulating around the classroom while students work either individually or in small groups. Carefully attending to what students do as they work makes it possible for teachers to use their observations to decide what and whom to focus on during the discussion that follows (Lampert 2001).

One way to facilitate the monitoring process is for the teacher, before beginning the lesson, to create a list of solutions that he or she anticipates that students will produce and that will help in accomplishing his or her mathematical goals for the lesson. The list, such as the one shown in column 1 of the chart in figure 1.1 for the Leaves and Caterpillars task, can help the teacher keep track of which students or groups produced which solutions or brought out which ideas that he or she wants to make sure to capture during the whole-group discussion. The "Other" cell in the first column provides the teacher with the opportunity to capture ideas that he or she had *not* anticipated.

Strategy	Who and What	Order
Unit rate Find the number of leaves eaten by one caterpillar (2.5) and multiply by 12 or add the amount for one 12 times	Janine – multiplied 12 × 2.5 (sticks representing caterpillars) Kyra – added 2.5 12 times (picture of leaves and caterpillars)	
Scale Factor Find that the number of caterpillars (12) is 6 times the original amount (2), so the number of leaves (30) must be 6 times the original amount (5)	Jason – narrative description	
Scaling Up Increasing the number of leaves and caterpillars by continuing to add 5 to the leaves and 2 to the caterpillars, until you reach the desired number of caterpillars	Jamal – table with leaves and caterpillars increasing in increments of 2 and 5	
Additive Find that the number of caterpillars has increased by 10 (2 + 10 = 12), so the number of leaves must also increase by 10 (5 + 10 = 15)	Missy and Kate	
Other Scaling up by collecting sets of 2 leaves and 5 caterpillars	Martin (picture) Melissa (table)	

Fig. 1.1. A chart for monitoring students' work on the Leaves and Caterpillars task

As discussed in the introduction, Mr. Crane's lesson provided limited, if any, evidence of active monitoring. Although Mr. Crane knew who got correct answers and who did not and that a range of strategies had been used, his choice of students to present at the end of the class suggests that he had not monitored the specific mathematical learning potential available in any of the responses. What Mr. Crane could have done while students worked on the task is shown in the second column in the chart in figure 1.1.

It is important to note, however, that monitoring involves more than just watching and listening to students. During this time, the teacher should also ask questions that will make students' thinking visible, help students clarify their thinking, ensure that members of the group are all engaged in the activity, and press students to consider aspects of the task to which they need to attend. Many of these questions can be planned in advance of the lesson, on the basis of the anticipated solutions. For example, if Mr. Crane had anticipated that a student would use a unit-rate approach (Janine's or Kyra's responses—see fig. 1.2), reasoning from the fact that the number of leaves eaten by one caterpillar was 2.5, then he might have been prepared to question, say, for example, Janine, regarding how she came up with the number 2.5 and how she knew to multiply it by 12. Questioning a student or group of students while they are exploring the task provides them with the opportunity to refine or revise their strategy prior to whole-group discussion and provides the teacher with insights regarding what the student understands about the problem and the mathematical ideas embedded in it.

Selecting

Having monitored the available student strategies in the class, the teacher can then select particular students to share their work with the rest of the class to get specific mathematics into the open for examination, thus giving the teacher more control over the discussion (Lampert 2001). The selection of particular students and their solutions is guided by the mathematical goal for the lesson and the teacher's assessment of how each contribution will contribute to that goal. Thus, the teacher selects certain students to present because of the mathematics in their responses.

A typical way to accomplish "selection" is to call on specific students (or groups of students) to present their work as the discussion proceeds. Alternatively, the teacher may let students know before the discussion that they will be presenting their work. In a hybrid variety, a teacher might ask for volunteers but then select a particular student that he or she knows is one of several who have a particularly useful idea to share with the class. By calling for volunteers but then strategically selecting from among them, the teacher signals appreciation for students' spontaneous contributions, while at the same time keeping control of the ideas that are publicly presented.

Returning to the Leaves and Caterpillar vignette, if we look at the strategies that were shared, we note that Kyra and Janine had similar strategies that used the idea of unit rate (i.e., finding out the number of leaves needed for one caterpillar). Given that, there may not have been any added mathematical value to sharing both. In fact, if Mr. Crane wanted to students to see the multiplicative nature of the relationship, he might have selected Janine, since her approach clearly involved multiplication.

Also, there might have been some payoff from sharing the solution produced by Missy and Kate (fig. 0.1) and contrasting it with the solution produced by Melissa (fig. 0.2). Although both approaches used addition, Missy and Kate inappropriately added the same number (10) to both the leaves and the caterpillars. Melissa, on the other hand, added 5 leaves for every 2 caterpillars, illustrating that she understood that this ratio (5 for every 2) had to be kept constant.

Sequencing

Having selected particular students to present, the teacher can then make decisions regarding how to sequence the student presentations. By making purposeful choices about the order in which students' work is shared, teachers can maximize the chances of achieving their mathematical goals for the discussion. For example, the teacher might want to have the strategy used by the majority of students presented before those that only a few students used, to validate the work that the majority of students did and make the beginning of the discussion accessible to as many students as possible. Alternatively, the teacher might want to begin with a strategy that is more concrete (using drawings or concrete materials) and move to strategies that are more abstract (using algebra). This approach—moving from concrete to abstract—serves to validate less sophisticated approaches and allows for connections among approaches. If a common misconception underlies a strategy that several students used, the teacher might want to have it addressed first so that the class can clear up that misunderstanding to be able to work on developing more successful ways of tackling the problem. Finally, the teacher might want to have related or contrasting strategies presented one right after the other in order to make it easier for the class to compare them. Again, during planning the teacher can consider possible ways of sequencing anticipated responses to highlight the mathematical ideas that are key to the lesson. Unanticipated responses can then be fitted into the sequence as the teacher makes final decisions about what is going to be presented.

More research needs to be done to compare the value of different sequencing methods, but we want to emphasize here that particular sequences can be used to advance particular goals for a lesson. Returning to the Leaves and Caterpillar vignette, we point out one sequence that could have been used: Martin (scaling up by collecting sets—picture), Jamal (scaling up—table), Janine (unit rate—picture/written explanation); and Jason (scale factor—written explanation).

This ordering begins with the least sophisticated representation (a picture) of the least sophisticated strategy (scaling up by collecting sets) and ends with the most sophisticated strategy (scale factor), a sequencing that would help with the goal of accessibility. In addition, by having the same strategy (scaling up) embodied in two different representations (a picture and a table), students would have the opportunity to develop deeper understandings of how to think about this problem in terms of scaling up.

Connecting

Finally, the teacher helps students draw connections between their solutions and other students' solutions as well as the key mathematical ideas in the lesson. The teacher can help students to make judgments about the consequences of different approaches for the range of problems that can be solved, one's likely accuracy and efficiency in solving them, and the kinds of mathematical patterns that can be most easily discerned. Rather than having mathematical discussions consist of separate presentations of different ways to solve a particular problem, the goal is to have student presentations build on one another to develop powerful mathematical ideas.

Returning to Mr. Crane's class, let's suppose that the sequencing of student presentations was Martin, Jamal, Janine, and Jason, as discussed above. Students could be asked to compare Jamal and Janine's responses and to identify where Janine's unit rate (2.5 leaves per caterpillar) is found in Jamal's table (it is the factor by which the number of caterpillars must be multiplied to get the number of leaves). Students could also be asked to compare Jason's explanation with Jamal and Martin's work to see if the scale factor of 6 can be seen in each of their tabular and pictorial representations.

It is important to note that the five practices build on another. Monitoring is less daunting if the teacher has taken the time to anticipate ways in which students might solve a task. Although a teacher cannot know with 100 percent certainty how students will solve a problem prior to the lesson, many solutions can be anticipated and thus easily recognized during monitoring. A teacher who has already thought about the mathematics represented by those solutions can turn his or her attention to making mathematical sense of those solutions that are unanticipated. Selecting, sequencing, and connecting, in turn, build on effective monitoring. Effective monitoring will yield the substance for a discussion that builds on student thinking, yet moves assuredly toward the mathematical goal of the lesson.

Conclusion

The purpose of the five practices is to provide teachers with more control over student-centered pedagogy. They do so by allowing the teacher to manage the content that will be discussed and how it will be discussed. Through careful planning, the amount of improvisation required by the teacher "in the moment" is kept to a minimum. Thus, teachers are freed up to listen to and make sense of outlier strategies and to thoughtfully plan connections between different ways of solving problems. All of this leads to more coherent, yet student-focused, discussions.

In the next chapter, we explore an important first step in enacting the five practices: setting goals for instruction and identifying appropriate tasks. Although this work is not one of the five practices, it is the foundation on which the five practices are built. In chapters 3, 4, and 5, we then explore the five practices in depth and provide additional illustrations showing what the practices look like when enacted and how the practices can lead to more productive discussions.

CHAPTER 2

Laying the Groundwork: Setting Goals and Selecting Tasks

To ensure that a discussion will be productive, teachers need to have clear learning goals for what they are trying to accomplish in the lesson, and they must select a task that has the potential to help students achieve those goals. In this chapter, we address these two components of planning for teaching to examine how they provide a critical foundation for effective discussions.

Setting Goals for Instruction

Specifying the mathematical goals for the lesson is a critical starting point for planning and teaching a lesson. In fact, some of the teachers with whom we have worked have argued that determining the mathematical goal for the lesson should be "practice 0," suggesting that it is the foundation on which the five practices are built. We agree that setting the goal for the lesson is indeed an a priori practice—it must occur before enacting the five practices. The key is to specify a goal that clearly identifies what students are to know and understand about mathematics as a result of their engagement in a particular lesson.

ACTIVE ENGAGEMENT 2.1
Figure 2.1 shows three statements of goals for a lesson on the Pythagorean theorem. Review the goal statements in the figure and consider the following questions:

- How are the goal statements the same, and how are they different?

- How might differences in goal statements matter?

Consider, for example, a lesson on the Pythagorean theorem for eighth-grade students. The goal for the lesson could be stated in several different ways, reflecting different levels of generality, as shown in the chart in figure 2.1. Goals A and B simply indicate what students will learn (goal A) and what students will do (goal B) but provide no insight into the mathematical understanding that they will develop during the lesson. It is unlikely that either goal A or goal B will provide much guidance to the teacher in select-ing instructional activities that will develop students' understanding of the conceptual basis for the theorem or in guiding and shaping students' understanding during the lesson.

Goal A: Students will learn the Pythagorean theorem ($c^2 = a^2 + b^2$).
Goal B: Students will be able to (SWBAT) use the Pythagorean theorem ($c^2 = a^2 + b^2$) to solve a series of missing value problems.
Goal C: Students will recognize that the area of the square built on the hypotenuse of a right triangle is equal to the sum of the areas of the squares built on the legs and will conjecture that $c^2 = a^2 + b^2$.

Fig. 2.1. Three different goal statements for a lesson on the Pythagorean theorem

By contrast, goal C explicitly states the mathematical relationship that is at the heart of the Pythagorean theorem—that the area of the square built on the hypotenuse of a right triangle is equal to the sum of the areas of the squares built on the legs. The specificity of this goal provides the teacher with a clear instructional target that can guide the selection of activities and the use of the five practices discussed in chapter 1. Hiebert and colleagues (2007, p. 51) argue that this level of specificity is critical to effective teaching:

> Without explicit learning goals, it is difficult to know what counts as evidence of students' learning, how students' learning can be linked to particular instructional activities, and how to revise instruction to facilitate students' learning more effec-tively. Formulating clear, explicit learning goals sets the stage for everything else.

Now consider again the lesson taught by David Crane, discussed previously in the introduction and chapter 1. Without a clear goal for what students were to learn during the lesson, the discussion failed to highlight any key mathematical ideas or relationships. This shortcoming raises questions re-garding what students learned and how Mr. Crane could assess their learning. Suppose, by contrast, that the goal for the lesson was for students to recognize that the relationship between caterpillars and leaves was multiplicative, not additive—that the leaves and caterpillars need to grow at a con-stant rate (for every 2 two caterpillars, there are 5 leaves; for each caterpillar, there are 2.5 leaves). This goal would provide a clear target for discussion, helping the teacher decide which solutions to highlight and what questions to ask about the solutions.

ACTIVE ENGAGEMENT 2.2
Consider a lesson that you have recently taught, in which the learning goal was not explicit.

- Rewrite the learning goal so that the mathematical idea that you wanted students to learn is explicit.

- How might your more explicit goal statement influence the way in which you plan or teach the lesson?

Being clear about the mathematical ideas that will be the target of instruction can be challenging. Teachers often think of lessons in relation to the activities that they will ask students to do rather than what students will come to know and understand about mathematics as a result of having engaged in the lesson. Textbooks that are used in mathematics methods courses intended for preservice teachers can be useful resources in helping teachers unpack learning goals in ways that highlight the mathematical ideas to be learned. For example, in *Elementary and Middle School Mathematics: Teaching Developmentally* (Van De Walle, Karp, and Bay-Williams 2010), the authors identify a set of big ideas for each content chapter, make clear how understanding of the big ideas develops, and provide tasks that can be used to help students develop this understanding. In addition, the teachers' editions of some K–12 textbooks provide similar support. For example, in *Connected Mathematics* (Lappan et al. 2010), the authors provide a list of the big ideas in a unit and articulate how each investigation contributes to the development of the identified ideas.

Selecting an Appropriate Task

Different tasks provide different opportunities for student learning. Tasks that ask students to perform a memorized procedure in a routine manner lead to one type of opportunity for student thinking; tasks that demand engagement with concepts and that stimulate students to make connections lead to a different set of opportunities for student thinking. Consider the two versions of a task shown in figure 2.2.

Task A	Task B
MAKING CONJECTURES—Complete the conjecture based on the pattern you observe in the specific cases. **29. Conjecture:** The sum of any two odd numbers is _____. $1 + 1 = 2$ $7 + 11 = 18$ $1 + 3 = 4$ $13 + 19 = 32$ $3 + 5 = 8$ $201 + 305 = 506$ **30. Conjecture:** The product of any two odd numbers is _____. $1 \times 1 = 1$ $7 \times 11 = 77$ $1 \times 3 = 3$ $13 \times 19 = 247$ $3 \times 5 = 15$ $201 \times 305 = 61,305$ (From Larson, Boswell, and Stiff [2004, p. 7].)	For problems 29 and 30, complete the conjecture on the basis of the pattern that you observe in the examples. Then explain why the conjecture is always true or show a case in which it is not true. **29. Conjecture:** The sum of any two odd numbers is _____. $1 + 1 = 2$ $7 + 11 = 18$ $1 + 3 = 4$ $13 + 19 = 32$ $3 + 5 = 8$ $201 + 305 = 506$ **30. Conjecture:** The product of any two odd numbers is _____. $1 \times 1 = 1$ $7 \times 11 = 77$ $1 \times 3 = 3$ $13 \times 19 = 247$ $3 \times 5 = 15$ $201 \times 305 = 61,305$

Fig. 2.2. Two versions of the odd number task

Although at first glance tasks A and B seem quite similar (both tasks ask students to make a conjecture about odd numbers based on empirical examples), the tasks are quite different in terms of the level of thinking required of the student. In task A, students need only notice that all of the answers are even (in the case of addition) or odd (in the case of multiplication) and then complete the conjecture accordingly.

The task does not press them to figure out why the particular pattern works in the way that it does. The task requires minimal thinking and reasoning. Therefore, task A would be considered low level. In task B, students are asked to explain why the conjecture is true. In other words, students need to figure out why this conjecture holds across the set of examples. Explaining why a conjecture is always true presses students to dig into the mathematics underlying the observed pattern. As a result, task B can be viewed as high level. There is no prescribed way of solving the task, and hence it requires students to think about what they know about odd numbers and how to use this knowledge to create a reasonable explanation.

The Task Analysis Guide (Smith and Stein 1998), shown in figure 2.3, provides a general list of characteristics of low-level (left side of the figure) and high-level (right side of the figure) mathematical tasks and thus can be used to analyze the potential of tasks to support students' thinking and reasoning. The guide is intended to help teachers match tasks with their goals for student learning.

Lower-level demands	Higher-level demands
Memorization • Involve either reproducing previously learned facts, rules, formulas, or definitions or committing facts, rules, formulas, or definitions to memory • Cannot be solved by using procedures, because a procedure does not exist or because the time frame in which the task is being completed is too short to use a procedure • Are not ambiguous. Such tasks involve exact reproduction of previously seen material, and what is to be reproduced is clearly and directly stated. • Have no connection to the concepts or meaning that underlies the facts, rules, formulas, or definitions being learned or reproduced	Procedures with connections • Focus students' attention on the use of procedures for the purpose of developing deeper levels of understanding of mathematical concepts and ideas • Suggest, explicitly or implicitly, pathways to follow that are broad general procedures that have close connections to underlying conceptual ideas as opposed to narrow algorithms that are opaque with respect to underlying concepts • Usually are represented in multiple ways, such as visual diagrams, manipulatives, symbols, and problem situations. Making connections among multiple representations helps develop meaning. • Require some degree of cognitive effort. Although general procedures may be followed, they cannot be followed mindlessly. Students need to engage with conceptual ideas that underlie the procedures to complete the task successfully and that develop understanding.
Procedures without connections • Are algorithmic. Use of the procedure is either specifically called for or is evident from prior instruction, experience, or placement of the task. • Require limited cognitive demand for successful completion. Little ambiguity exists about what needs to be done or how to do it. • Have no connection to the concepts or meaning that underlies the procedure being used • Are focused on producing correct answers instead of on developing mathematical understanding • Require no explanations or explanations that focus solely on describing the procedure that was used	Doing mathematics • Require complex and nonalgorithmic thinking—a predictable, well-rehearsed approach or pathway is not explicitly suggested by the task, task instructions, or a worked-out example • Require students to explore and understand the nature of mathematical concepts, processes, or relationships • Demand self-monitoring or self-regulation of one's own cognitive processes • Require students to access relevant knowledge and experiences and make appropriate use of them in working through the task • Require students to analyze the task and actively examine task constraints that may limit possible solution strategies and solutions • Require considerable cognitive effort and may involve some level of anxiety for the student because of the unpredictable nature of the solution process required

Note: These characteristics of mathematical instructional tasks are derived from the work of Doyle (1988) on academic tasks, Resnick (1987) on high-level thinking skills, and the examination and categorization of hundreds of tasks used in QUASAR classrooms (Stein, Grover, and Henningsen 1996; Stein, Lane, and Silver 1996).

Fig. 2.3. The Task Analysis Guide. (From Smith and Stein [1998].)

ACTIVE ENGAGEMENT 2.3

Use the Task Analysis Guide to analyze the tasks that you have used in one of your classes over the last few weeks.

- To what extent did you provide your students with the opportunity to engage in high-level tasks?

- Can you identify tasks in your textbook that would provide additional opportunities for students to think and reason (processes on the right side of the Task Analysis Guide)?

It is critical that the task that a teacher selects align with the goals of the lesson. Consider the corresponding goals and tasks in figure 2.4. If, for example, the goal of a lesson is for students to use the Pythagorean theorem to find the value of a, b, or c (goal B in fig. 2.4), then a set of procedural exercises (shown on the right side of the figure) in which students find missing values for a, b, and c by substituting the given values into the formula has the potential to accomplish the goal. However, if the goal is for students to recognize that the area of the square built on the hypotenuse of a right triangle is equal to the sum of the areas of the squares built on the legs and conjecture that $c^2 = a^2 + b^2$ (goal C in fig. 2.4), then a different task would be needed.

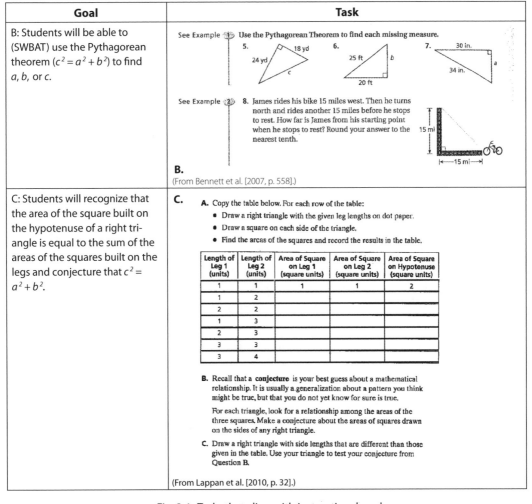

Fig. 2.4. Tasks that align with instructional goals

Task B is a *procedures without connections* task (see the lower left quadrant of the Task Analysis Guide in fig. 2.3), which requires the application of a known procedure. It is important to note that even though question 8 in task B is a word problem (often considered high level because such problems are difficult for students), the drawing that is provided and the reference to an example make this task no more than a procedural exercise.

By contrast, goal C requires a task that provides students with the opportunity to explore the relationship among squares built on the sides of a right triangle. Task C in figure 2.4 provides such an opportunity. By drawing right triangles with sides of different lengths, building squares on the sides, and finding and recording the areas, students are able to look for patterns in the data that they have gathered and make a conjecture about the relationship among the areas of the squares that they have drawn. Task C may be considered a *procedures with connections* task (see the upper right quadrant of the Task Analysis Guide in fig. 2.3), since students are given a broad procedure for solving the problem (draw right triangles, draw squares on the sides of the triangle, find the area of the squares, record the data in a table), but students must analyze the data in the table and determine the relationship among the areas of the squares. Through this process, students are positioned to see the connection between the formula and the underlying meaning.

Another important consideration in selecting a task is the extent to which the task permits entry to students who bring with them a range of prior knowledge and experience. This is a critical factor in ensuring equity in the classroom. For example, if a task asks students to do or explore something (e.g., task C in fig. 2.4), students equipped with appropriate resources (e.g., dot paper or geoboards) should be able to get a foothold that will move them toward a solution, and this could serve as a starting point for a conversation. However, if a task asks a student to solve a set of exercises that require the application of a particular rule (e.g., task B in fig. 2.4) and the student does not know the rule (e.g., that $c^2 = a^2 + b^2$), the student has no recourse—there is nothing to be done—other than to ask for assistance from the teacher or simply disengage from the activity altogether.

ACTIVE ENGAGEMENT 2.4
Figure 2.5 shows the Tiling a Patio task. See how many different but equivalent rules you can find in part *d*.

Equity can also be achieved when students are given tasks that can be solved or represented in different ways. Figure 2.5, for example, shows the Tiling a Patio task, which would be classified as *doing mathematics* (see the lower right quadrant of the Task Analysis Guide in fig. 2.3). Students could begin work on this task in several ways: build additional patios by using tiles in two colors, draw subsequent patios on grid paper and count the number of border tiles, make a table that shows the patio number and the number of tiles in the border and look for patterns, or just notice the recursive "+2" pattern. Hence, it is likely that all students will be able to *enter* the task (i.e., do something mathematical). As Smith, Hillen, and Catania (2007, p. 40) note, gaining entry into a task is the starting point for a teachers' work:

Once a student has a foothold on solving the task, the teacher is then positioned to ask questions to assess what the student understands about the relationships in the task and to advance students beyond their starting point.

Tiling a Patio

Alfredo Gomez is designing patios. Each patio has a rectangular garden area in the center. Alfredo uses black tiles to represent the soil of the garden. Around each garden, he designs a border of white tiles. The pictures shown below show the three smallest patios that he can design with black tiles for the garden and white tiles for the border.

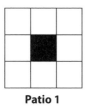   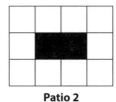   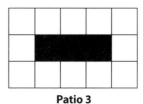

       Patio 1   **Patio 2**   **Patio 3**

a. Draw patio 4 and patio 5. How many white tiles are in patio 4? Patio 5?

b. Make some observations about the patios that could help you describe larger patios.

c. Describe a method for finding the total number of white tiles needed for patio 50 (without constructing it).

d. Write a rule that could be used to determine the number of white tiles needed for any patio. Explain how your rule relates to the visual representation of the patio.

e. Write a different rule that could be used to determine the number of white tiles needed for any patio. Explain how your rule relates to the visual representation of the patio.

Fig. 2.5. The Tiling a Patio task. (Adapted from Cuevas and Yeatts [2005, pp. 18–22].)

In addition, if the task asked students only to write a rule (part *d* in fig. 2.5), the students who struggle to use symbolic notation would have little recourse and the teacher would have limited insight into what they could do and what they were struggling to understand. Because the task scaffolds students' work from drawing patios with small numbers of tiles, to making observations about the patios, to describing the number of border tiles for a patio too large to build or draw, students are able to concentrate on describing the relationship between the number of border tiles and the patio number before having to model it symbolically. Hence, students can demonstrate that they were able to identify and describe the relationships with words—a key first step in the process of writing a symbolic rule.

Conclusion

To have a productive mathematical discussion, teachers must first establish a clear and specific goal with respect to the mathematics to be learned and then select a high-level mathematical task (i.e., a task that meets the criteria specified on the right-hand side of the Task Analysis Guide in fig. 2.3). This is not to say that all tasks that are selected and used in the classroom must be high level, but rather that productive discussions that highlight key mathematical ideas are unlikely to occur if the task on which students are working requires limited thinking and reasoning.

In the next chapter, we will explore an instructional episode in which an eighth-grade teacher uses the Tiling a Patio task as the basis for a lesson on linear functions. Through this exploration, we will consider the alignment of the goals that the teacher set for student learning and the selected task and determine the extent to which the teacher used the five practices to facilitate students' learning opportunities during the lesson.

CHAPTER 3

Investigating the Five Practices in Action

In chapter 1, we presented the five practices for orchestrating a productive discussion and considered what David Crane's class *might* have looked like had he engaged in these practices and how use of the practices in advance of and during the lesson *could* have had an impact on students' opportunities to learn mathematics. In this chapter, we analyze the teaching of Darcy Dunn, an eighth-grade teacher who has spent several years trying to improve the quality of discussions in her classroom.

The Five Practices in the Case of Darcy Dunn

The vignette that follows, Tiling a Patio: The Case of Darcy Dunn, provides an opportunity to consider the extent to which the teacher appears to have engaged in some or all of the five practices before or during the featured lesson and the ways in which her use of the practices may have contributed to students' opportunities to learn. (This case, written by Smith, Hillen, and Catania [2007], is based on observed instruction in the third author's classroom.)

ACTIVE ENGAGEMENT 3.1
Read the vignette Tiling a Patio: The Case of Darcy Dunn and identify places in the lesson where Ms. Dunn appears to be engaging in the five practices. Use the line numbers to help you keep track of the places where you think she used each practice.

Tiling a Patio: The Case of Darcy Dunn
Darcy Dunn was working on a unit on functions with her eighth-grade students early in the school year and decided to engage them in solving the Tiling a Patio task [shown previously as fig. 2.3 but repeated here as fig. 3.1 for the reader's convenience]. As a

result of this lesson, she wanted her students to understand three mathematical
ideas: (1) that linear functions grow at a constant rate; (2) that there are different but equivalent ways of writing an explicit rule that defines the relationship
between two variables; and (3) that the rate of change of a linear function can
be highlighted in different representational forms: as the successive difference in
a table of (x, y) values in which values for x increase by 1, as the m value in the
equation $y = mx + b$, and as the slope of the function when graphed.

Alfredo Gomez is designing patios. Each patio has a rectangular garden area in the center. Alfredo uses black tiles to represent the soil of the garden. Around each garden, he designs a border of white tiles. The pictures shown below show the three smallest patios that he can design with black tiles for the garden and white tiles for the border.

 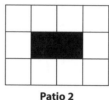 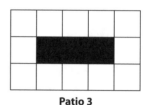

Patio 1   **Patio 2**   **Patio 3**

a. Draw patio 4 and patio 5. How many white tiles are in patio 4? Patio 5?

b. Make some observations about the patios that could help you describe larger patios.

c. Describe a method for finding the total number of white tiles needed for patio 50 (without constructing it).

d. Write a rule that could be used to determine the number of white tiles needed for any patio. Explain how your rule relates to the visual representation of the patio.

e. Write a different rule that could be used to determine the number of white tiles needed for any patio. Explain how your rule relates to the visual representation of the patio.

Fig. 3.1. The Tiling a Patio task. (Adapted from Cuevas and Yeatts [2005, pp. 18–22].)

In addition to the fact that the task provided a context for exploring the
mathematical ideas that Ms. Dunn had targeted, it had an aspect that she found
particularly appealing: all students, regardless of prior knowledge and experiences,
would have access to the task. Every student would be able to build or draw the
next two patios (part a) and make some observations about the patios (part b).
Although finding the number of white (border) tiles in patio 50 (part c) would be
more challenging, students could make a table and look for numeric patterns or
"see" one of the many relationships between the white and black tiles in the diagram itself.

Ms. Dunn began the lesson by having a student read the task aloud and making sure that all of the students understood what the problem was asking. She told
students that they would have five minutes of "private think time" to begin working on the problem individually and reminded them to help themselves to any of
the materials (tiles, grid paper, colored pencils, calculators) on their tables. They
could then share their ideas about the task with the other members of their table
groups and work together to come up with a solution.

As students worked on the task, first on their own and later in collaboration with their peers, Ms. Dunn circulated among the groups, making note of the different approaches that students were using, asking clarifying questions, and pressing the students to think about what the bigger patios would "look like" and how they could figure that out without building or drawing them all. She noted that although all the groups were able to complete parts *a* and *b*, a few students, such as James, were having difficulty describing patio 50, and many were struggling to write symbolic rules for part *d*. Through her questioning during small-group work, these struggling students had made some progress, and she decided that the students could continue working on providing verbal descriptions and converting them to symbolic rules as a whole class.

After about fifteen minutes of small-group work, Ms. Dunn decided that she would ask Beth to present her group's strategy first for part *d*. Several groups had used the same approach, but it had been several days since Beth had contributed to a whole-class discussion in a central way, and Ms. Dunn wanted this quiet student to have a chance to demonstrate her competence. As Beth approached the overhead projector in the front of the room, Ms. Dunn handed her a few overhead pens in different colors and one of the transparencies that she had prepared in advance, showing the first three patios. This way, Beth could easily explain what she did and how it connected to the drawing without having to draw all the patios. The following dialogue ensued between Beth and Ms. Dunn:

Beth:	You multiply by two and add six.
Ms. Dunn:	You multiply *what* by two?
Beth:	The black tiles.
Ms. Dunn:	Write it down somewhere. You multiply the black tiles by two, and then add six. Can you show us on the diagram—where do you see it on the picture? Where do you see that, to multiply by two? You can write on the transparency.
Beth:	*[Demonstrating her method on the drawing of patio 1]* There's one, then one tile times two equals two, plus six, equals eight, and then, it's eight tiles.
Ms. Dunn:	OK, you add six. Where is the constant of six?
Beth:	Because there's three on each side.
Ms. Dunn:	Circle them for me.
Beth:	*[Makes circles around the tiles on the sides of patio 1, as shown in fig. 3.2a.]*
Ms. Dunn:	One, and the two—where's the two? Two ones are where?
Beth:	Right there, and right there *[points to the middle tile of the three tiles on the top row and the bottom row of patio 1, as shown in fig. 3.2b.]*

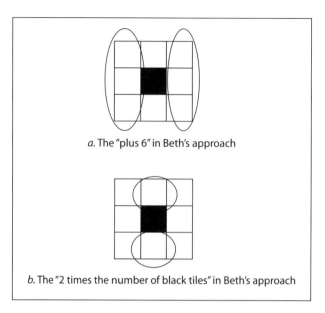

a. The "plus 6" in Beth's approach

b. The "2 times the number of black tiles" in Beth's approach

Fig. 3.2. Beth's approach to patio 1

After Beth's presentation, Ms. Dunn pressed students to express Beth's way of viewing the pattern symbolically as $w = 2b + 6$, where w is the number of white tiles in the patio and b is the number of black tiles. Sherrill commented that the number of black tiles was the same as the patio number, so it didn't matter if they used b (for black tiles) or p (for patio number). Ms. Dunn asked Sherrill to write the generalization for the number of tiles on the newsprint that was hanging on the board so that everyone could keep track of the different ways of finding the total number of white tiles in any patio.

Ms. Dunn then asked for a second method from the class. Several students volunteered to present their work, and after quickly checking the notes that she had made as she had monitored the small-group work, Ms. Dunn selected Faith to go next. On a new transparency, Faith demonstrated her approach to patio 1 [shown in fig. 3.3], explaining, "I did the number of black tiles, and I added two [see step 1 in fig. 3.3]. You do that times two to get the top and bottom [see step 2 in fig. 3.3]. Then I did plus two" [see step 3 in fig. 3.3].

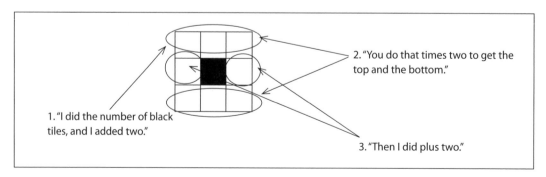

2. "You do that times two to get the top and the bottom."

1. "I did the number of black tiles, and I added two."

3. "Then I did plus two."

Fig. 3.3. Faith's explanation of her approach on patio 1

When Faith had finished her explanation, Ms. Dunn commented, "OK, I don't think everyone understood that. Does anyone have a question for Faith?" Pedro was the first to raise his hand, and Ms. Dunn encouraged Faith to call on him. Pedro asked, "Where did your last 'plus two' come from?" Faith clarified, "These two right here [pointing to the white tiles to the left and right of the black tile in patio 1], because they're the two remaining tiles that you haven't added already."

Ms. Dunn then asked the class how they could write an equation for Faith's approach. Damien volunteered that his group had thought about the problem in the same way that Faith did, and they had come up with the equation $w = 2(b + 2) + 2$. At the teacher's request, Damien went to the front of the room to explain why this equation worked, using the drawing of patio 3. He explained, "The number of black tiles (or the patio number) plus two will always give you the top and bottom rows, and then you always have one on each side which gives you the plus two." Ms. Dunn asked Damien to add the equation to the newsprint list.

Ms. Dunn then asked Devon if he would be willing to share his approach. Time was running out, and Ms. Dunn wanted to make sure that his approach, which focused on finding the total area of the rectangular region (the patio plus the garden) and then subtracting out the area of the garden, was made public, since it was different from other approaches and had the potential to be a useful strategy for solving problems that students would encounter in the future. Ms. Dunn engaged Devon in the following dialogue:

Devon: OK, like Damien was saying, there's always going to be two more tiles on the bottom [row].

Ms. Dunn: Draw on it [*hands Damien a transparency*].

Devon: [*Drawing and explaining*] There's always going to be two more tiles down here [*see step 1 in fig. 3.4*] than there is right here. So, I knew that in patio 50 there was going to be fifty-two on the bottom, 'cause there's fifty black tiles. And, so I took fifty-two times three, these three [*pointing*], 'cause there's always three on the side [*see step 2 in fig. 3.4*], no matter what patio it is, and I got a hundred fifty-six. Which gives you the area; then you subtract the black ones [*see step 3 in fig. 3.4*], so you subtract fifty and that gives you a hundred and six.

Ms. Dunn: Oh! That was pretty creative. He took the whole figure, and then subtracted out the area in the middle. Ooh—I like it.

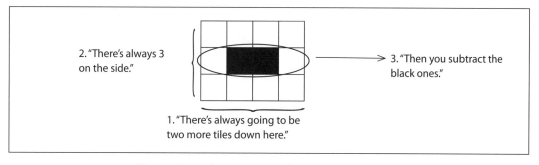

Fig. 3.4. Devon's explanation of his approach to patio 2

120 Ms. Dunn then asked the class how they could write Devon's rule, using symbols. Phoebe said that it would be $w = 3(b + 2) - b$. James had a puzzled look on his face, and Ms. Dunn asked him if he had a question for Phoebe. James asked, "Why did you multiply by 3? Everyone else multiplied by 2." Phoebe responded, "Devon is using all three rows of the patio, so he has three rows of $p + 2$, not two rows like Faith had. But then, you have to subtract the black part 'cause it isn't part of the patio." James said, "So you took times three and subtracted, while

125 Faith did times two and added. I get it."

Ms. Dunn very much wanted students to consider the table that Tamika had built when she started the problem. She thought that this representation, which included the first ten patios, would help students see that the number of white tiles increased by 2 as the patio number increased by 1 (that is, that the rate of

130 change is 2)—an idea that had not been salient in any of the presentations so far. Ms. Dunn then planned to ask students to show where this "+2" was in the picture and in the equation. She wanted to make sure that they saw the connection among the picture, the table, and the equation. She then wanted to have students predict what the graph would look like and why, and, ultimately, graph it. But

135 she knew that this work could not be done in the remaining five minutes of class. Instead, she decided that she would begin tomorrow's class with a discussion of the table and the graph.

Ms. Dunn decided to use the limited time she had left to return to the list of equations that the students had produced during the discussion, to which Phoebe

140 had added the last equation. She called the students' attention to the list that was hanging in the front of the room [shown in fig. 3.5] and noted, "We came up with three different ways to find the total number of white tiles in any patio. Can they all be right?" She then asked students to spend the next few minutes discussing this question in their groups. Their homework assignment was to provide a

145 written answer to the question and to justify their conclusion.

$w = 2b + 6$ (Beth and class)
$w = 2(b + 2) + 2$ (Faith and Damien)
$w = 3(b + 2) - b$ (Devon and Phoebe)

In each equation, b is the number of black tiles (or p could be used instead as the patio number) and w is the number of white tiles in the patio.

Fig. 3.5. List of rules for determining the number of white tiles in any patio

Analyzing the Case of Darcy Dunn

Although we could identify many aspects of the instruction in Ms. Dunn's classroom that may have contributed to her students' opportunities to learn mathematics, we will focus our attention specifically on her use of the five practices. In subsequent chapters, we will analyze a broader set of actions that, in combination with the five practices, help account for the success of the lesson. We begin by considering the five practices and whether there is evidence that the teacher engaged in some or all of these practices. Then we consider how Ms. Dunn's use of the practices may have enhanced her students' opportunities to learn.

Evidence of the five practices

As we indicated in chapter 2, determining clear and specific mathematical goals for the lesson and selecting a task that aligns with the goals are the foundation on which the five practices are built. Hence, Darcy Dunn's identification of the three mathematical ideas that she wanted her students to learn (lines 5–10) and her selection of a task that had the potential to reach these goals (fig. 3.1 and lines 11–14) positioned her to use the five practices model effectively.

Anticipating

Because the vignette focuses primarily on what happened *during* a classroom episode, we have limited insight into the planning in which Darcy Dunn engaged prior to the lesson and the extent to which she anticipated specific solutions to the task. However, the fact that she wanted students to know that the rate of change of a linear function can be highlighted in different representational forms suggests that she had considered the possibilities for solving the task by using a table, an equation, and a graph (lines 7–10). In addition, Darcy's decision to begin the next class with a discussion of a table and a graph suggests that she considered these approaches and their usefulness in accomplishing her goal for the lesson. We might also argue that Darcy's goal to have students recognize that there are different but equivalent ways of writing an explicit rule that defines the relationship between two variables (lines 5–7) suggests that she had probably considered different rules for relating white and black tiles before she ever set foot in the classroom.

Monitoring

Ms. Dunn monitored students working individually and in their small groups (lines 27–37). Through this monitoring she was able to determine the approaches that specific students were using (lines 28–34), ask questions to help students make progress on the task (lines 34–35), and identify what students were struggling with (lines 31–34). Her monitoring of the students' work provided the information that she needed about their mathematical thinking to modify her lesson to meet their needs and to make a decision about which strategies and solutions to focus on during the discussion. Specifically, several students were having trouble connecting verbal descriptions with symbolic rules, and as a result Ms. Dunn decided to work on this translation issue with the entire class (lines 35–37).

Selecting

By referring to notes that she had made during the monitoring process (lines 27–37), Ms. Dunn knew which students had produced specific solutions. Armed with this information, she decided to have particular students (Beth, Faith, and Devon) present approaches to the task that would lead to different symbolic rules, thus providing students with additional experience in moving between verbal and symbolic notation. In addition, she decided that she wanted students to consider the table that Tamika had built (lines 126–30) so that they could see that the rate of change was +2 (i.e., that the number of white tiles increased by 2 as the patio number increased by 1). This would highlight the constant rate of change, one of her goals for the lesson (line 5).

Sequencing

Ms. Dunn selected Beth as the first presenter, since her strategy had been used by several groups and therefore was likely to be one to which other students in the class could readily relate (lines 38–40). In addition, she wanted to give Beth a chance to participate actively and publicly in class (lines 40–42) since it had been several days since she had done so. By selecting Beth, Ms. Dunn was able to both highlight a popular strategy and make sure that she was providing her students with equitable opportunities to demonstrate competence.

Although it might appear that Ms. Dunn's selection of Faith as the second presenter (lines 77–78) was a case of picking a volunteer, the fact that Ms. Dunn asked for a second method and then consulted her notes before selecting Faith (lines 75–78) suggests that the selection was strategic: Ms. Dunn was looking to see who among the volunteers had produced the strategy that she wanted to have presented. The strategy presented by Faith was a reasonable second choice since it was similar to the first strategy in that it counted only the white tiles and used the idea that there were two groups of tiles to be counted (Beth counted two groups—on the right and left side; Faith counted two groups—on the top and the bottom).

Ms. Dunn selected Devon to be the third presenter (line 97) because he had used an approach that was different from the others that had been presented up to this point, in that it focused on finding the area of the entire rectangular region and then subtracting the area of the black tiles to find the area of the white tiles. Hence, the strategy was different from the other two strategies in initially counting all the tiles, counting three groups rather than two groups, and using subtraction rather than addition. We might conclude that this strategy was not widely used within the class, and presenting other strategies first validated the thinking of the majority of students in the class and left them open to considering an alternative approach. In addition, presenting this strategy gave students access to an approach that could be useful on future tasks (lines 101–102).

Darcy's decision to present three solutions that were all verbal descriptions of the relationship between black and white tiles depicted in the diagram seems reasonable in light of the fact that students struggled to move from verbal descriptions to explicit rules. Working on the translation from words or written descriptions to symbols as a class provided students with additional support for representing quantities abstractly, a skill that would be critical as they moved forward in their study of functions.

In addition to the verbal or visual strategies described by Beth, Faith, and Devon, Darcy also planned to have Tamika discuss the table that she had created. She intended to use the table to highlight the rate of change (the ratio of the increase in patio number to the increase in white tiles) and to connect this with the diagram and equation.

Connecting

Through the questions that Ms. Dunn asked during the discussion and the ways in which she pressed students to clarify what they had done and why, she helped students make connections with the mathematical ideas that were the target of her instruction. Specifically, Ms. Dunn indicated that she wanted her students to be able recognize that (1) linear functions grow at a constant rate, (2) there are different but equivalent ways of writing an explicit rule that defines the relationship between two variables, and (3) the rate of change of a linear function can be highlighted in different representational forms.

Although the students struggled to write explicit rules on their own (goal 2), Ms. Dunn pressed them to translate the verbal descriptions given by Beth, Faith, and Devon into symbolic rules after each presentation (lines 67–69; 89–90; 118–19). By using the students' verbal descriptions, supported by diagrams, as a starting point, the teacher was able to help students achieve one of her goals for the lesson.

In addition, throughout the lesson, Ms. Dunn used the work produced by students to highlight the connections among different representations (goal 3). During each presentation, Ms. Dunn encouraged the students to connect the verbal description to the diagram through the use of drawings of patios that she provided and later to symbolic rules, as previously described.

Although the teacher did not make explicit connections among student solutions in the lesson, her discussion of Tamika's table the following day would position the class to connect the +2 in the table (the successive difference in the number of white tiles with each new patio) with Beth's verbal description and the related equation, as well as with the growth pattern for this function (goal 1). In addition, James's question to Phoebe (lines 120–21) provided an opportunity for students to connect the approaches used by Devon and Faith. Finally, the homework assignment given at the end of class would challenge students to consider how three different approaches could all be correct, although they looked quite different. This task could spark the notion that all three equations are equal to $w = 2b + 6$, produce the same output for the same input, and can be linked visually to the diagram of the patios.

Relating the five practices to learning opportunities

Did Darcy Dunn's use of the practices contribute to her students' learning? Although we have no direct evidence of what individuals in the class learned, we see a group of students who appear to be engaged in the learning process. Over the course of the lesson, the teacher involved eight different students in substantive ways. Ms. Dunn repeatedly targeted key ideas related to the goals of the lessons—writing explicit rules and connecting representations—as she guided her class in discussing three different solutions in depth. The final question that she gave for homework (lines 141–45) provided individual students with an opportunity to make sense of what had transpired during class and to make connections that would provide the teacher with insight into their thinking. Although the idea of a constant rate of change (goal 1) and that rate of change manifested itself differently across representations (goal 3) were not explicitly highlighted, the work that was done prepared the teacher and her students to explore these ideas in subsequent lessons.

The five practices gave the teacher a systematic approach to thinking through what her students might do with the task and how she could use their thinking to accomplish the goals that she had set. Although we analyzed the practices in action—what the teacher did during the lesson—we argue that to do what she did during the lesson, the teacher must have thought it all through *before* the lesson began. We will explore how to engage in such planning in subsequent chapters.

Conclusion

Darcy Dunn avoided a show-and-tell session in which solutions are presented in succession without much rhyme or reason, often obscuring the point of the lesson. By carefully considering the story line of her lesson—what she wanted to accomplish mathematically and how different strategies and representations would help her get there—she was able to question her students skillfully and position them to make key points. So, with the lesson always firmly under her control, the teacher was able to build on the work produced by students, carefully guiding them in a mathematically sound direction.

Consider, by contrast, the Leaves and Caterpillar vignette discussed in the introduction and chapter 1. Although the students in Mr. Crane's class used a range of interesting approaches, what the students were supposed to learn from the sequence of presentations was not clear, other than that "the problem could be solved in many different ways." The students took no clear mathematical message with them from this experience.

As we noted in chapter 1, the five practices build on each other, working in concert to support the orchestration of a productive discussion. It is the information gained from engaging in one practice that positions the teacher to engage in the subsequent practice. For example, you can't select solutions to be presented if you aren't aware of what students have produced (you need to monitor to be able to select and sequence); you can't make connections across strategies and to the mathematical goal of the lesson if you haven't first selected and sequenced strategies in a way that will help you make your point. In the next two chapters, we explore the five practices in more depth, building on the descriptions provided in chapter 1.

CHAPTER 4

Getting Started: Anticipating Students' Responses and Monitoring Their Work

O nce teachers have set a goal for instruction and identified an appropriate task on which students will work (as discussed in chapter 2), they are ready to begin work on the five practices. In this chapter, we discuss the first two practices—anticipating and monitoring—and consider what teachers can do prior to and during a lesson to position themselves to make productive use of student responses. By closely examining how one teacher engages in the first two practices, we can show how use of these practices *prior to* and *during* a lesson can set the stage for a productive discussion at the lesson's conclusion. In discussing each of the two practices, we first describe the practice, then present part of the case of a high school teacher, Nick Bannister, and then conclude with an analysis of this teacher's use of the practice. (Parts of this classroom vignette have been adapted from Bill and Jamar [2010] with permission from the University of Pittsburgh.)

Anticipating

Anticipating involves carefully considering (1) what strategies students are likely to use to approach or solve a challenging mathematical task (e.g., a high-level task), (2) how to respond to the work that students are likely to produce, and (3) which student strategies are likely to be most useful in addressing the mathematics to be learned. We will use the vignette Calling Plans: The Case of Nick Bannister (Part 1—Anticipating) to illustrate these three points.

ACTIVE ENGAGEMENT 4.1
Figure 4.1 shows the Calling Plans task.

- Solve the task in as many ways as you can, and consider other approaches that you think students might use to solve it.

- Identify errors or misconceptions that you would expect to emerge as students work on this task.

Calling Plans: The Case of Nick Bannister (Part 1—Anticipating)

Nick Bannister is beginning to work with his ninth-grade algebra 1 students on solving systems of equations. From the lesson he is currently planning, he wants his students to (1) recognize that there is a point of intersection between two unique nonparallel linear equations that represents where the two functions have the same *x*- and *y*-values; (2) understand that the two functions "switch positions" at the point of intersection and that the one that was on "top" before the point of intersection (more expensive in the calling plans context) is on the "bottom" after the point of intersection (less expensive in the calling plans context) because the function with the smaller rate of change will ultimately be the function closer to the *x*-axis; and (3) make connections between tables, graphs, equations, and context by identifying the slope and *y*-intercept in each representational form.

Nick decided to use the Calling Plans task, shown in figure 4.1, in this lesson because it provided a context for exploring systems of equations that would be of interest to students (who seem to spend far too much time on their cell phones) and therefore help them (he hoped!) in making sense of what the point of intersection means. He wanted to make sure that before he actually introduced procedures for finding the solution to a system (e.g., substitution and elimination) that his students had a firm grasp of what the solution means both graphically and contextually.

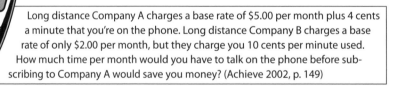

Long distance Company A charges a base rate of $5.00 per month plus 4 cents a minute that you're on the phone. Long distance Company B charges a base rate of only $2.00 per month, but they charge you 10 cents per minute used. How much time per month would you have to talk on the phone before subscribing to Company A would save you money? (Achieve 2002, p. 149)

Fig. 4.1. The Calling Plans task

Nick began planning the lesson by anticipating how students might solve the task. His first step in this process was to solve the problem himself by using non-procedural methods, since these were the methods to which his students would have access. He considered three general approaches, as shown in figure 4.2, as reasonable courses of action for his students.

Possible Solutions

Make a Table

Table A

Number of minutes	Cost A	Cost B	
0	5.00	2.00	
10	5.40	3.00	
20	5.80	4.00	
30	6.20	5.00	
40	6.60	6.00	
50	7.00	7.00	Same cost & min
60	7.40	8.00	

Because A is more than B at 40, the same as B at 50 and less than B at 60, A must become a better deal at 51 minutes.

Table B

Number of minutes	Cost A	Cost B	
0	5.00	2.00	
20	5.80	4.00	
40	6.60	6.00	A is more
60	7.40	8.00	A is less
80	8.20	10.00	
100	9.00	12.00	
120	9.80	14.00	

Because A is more than B at 40 and less than B at 60, the point of intersection must be somewhere between 40 and 60. If I graph them, I find that the point of intersection is 50. So A is a better deal starting at 51 minutes.

Write Equations

$y = 0.04x + 5$ (Company A)

$y = 0.10x + 2$ (Company B)

When I put the two equations into the graphing calculator, I found the point of intersection to be 50 minutes. So A becomes cheaper at 51 minutes.

Make a Graph

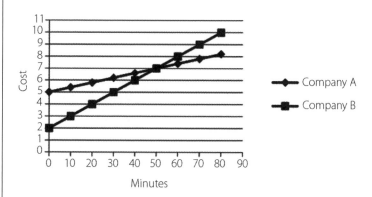

You can make a graph from a table of values by substituting two values for x into the equation and finding the corresponding values for y, or by putting either the table or the equation into the graphing calculator. No matter which approach you use, you find that the lines intersect at (50, 7), so plan A is better starting at 51 minutes.

Fig. 4.2. Nick Bannister's possible solutions

Nick predicted that many of his students would create tables, but he realized that they would not all would use increments of 10 minutes as he did in table A (in fig. 4.2). If students used 20-minute intervals, as he had done in table B (in the figure), or other increments that weren't factors of 50, Nick knew that they would not immediately see that the two plans had the same cost for 50 minutes. If this happened, he decided that he would draw students' attention to the rows in the table (e.g., 40 minutes and 60 minutes in table B) where the two plans changed position relative to each other (e.g., plan A was more expensive at 40 minutes but less expensive at 60 minutes, as shown in the two shades of gray in table B in fig. 4.2) and see if they could explain what was happening, and why, and if they could predict what the graph of the two equations would look like. He would then ask students to make a graph and see if it matched their prediction and helped them to answer the question. He also thought that students might not start their tables at 0, in which case he would ask students what it meant to talk for zero minutes and how much it would cost. He believed this was important, since zero minutes in this problem corresponded to the x-value of the y-intercept and gave the value of b when substituted into the equation in the form $y = mx + b$.

Nick thought that his students might be confused about several different aspects of the task, and he wanted to make sure that he was prepared to deal with these issues as they arose. For example, he thought that some students would write 4 cents as .4 or 4 rather than .04. In this case, he planned to ask students how they would write five dollars and four cents by using dollar-and-cent notation and have them compare that to what they now had. He didn't want to get sidetracked by these issues, but if students were calculating the cost with the wrong values, they were never going to get to the main point of the lesson. He wondered too if students might confuse the cost per minute and the monthly fee, producing an incorrect equation of $C = 4 + 5m$ for company A. In this case, he planned to ask students what 4 and 5 represented in the problem, which value changed as you talked more and which one didn't, what it would cost for 10 minutes by using their equation, and whether that made sense. Although he wanted students to be able to figure out their errors on their own, he wanted to be ready with some questions that would guide them in the right direction.

Nick wanted to make sure that when he got to the end of the lesson, he would have accomplished what he set out to do (i.e., students would recognize that the point of intersection is where two functions have the same x- and y-values, understand that the two functions "switch positions" at the point of intersection, and make connections among different representations) and to do so, he knew that he needed to have correct versions of all three representations—tables, graphs, and equations—available for the discussion. Because he wanted to build the discussion around the work that students produced, if at all possible, Nick decided to keep track of what students were doing as he observed and interacted with them as they worked on the task in small groups. To facilitate this process, he made a chart (shown in fig. 4.3) with rows for the student strategies that he was expecting to see (as well as a row for the unexpected) and columns to record who was doing what (i.e., which students or groups were using what strategies) during the lesson. (The chart also included a third column, labeled "Order," which Nick would use later, in connection with the next two practices, selecting and sequencing.) Nick thought the chart would help him in planning the discussion.

Strategy	Who and What	Order
Table		
Graph		
Equation		
Other		

Fig. 4.3. A chart for monitoring students' work on the Calling Plans task

ACTIVE ENGAGEMENT 4.2

Compare your response to Active Engagement 4.1 with the solutions and potential student errors that Nick Bannister generated.

Analysis of Anticipating in the Case of Nick Bannister

In the Case of Nick Bannister, we see a teacher who engaged in thoughtful planning for a lesson that he was going to teach in his ninth-grade algebra class. His planning started with the identification of clear goals for student learning (lines 3–11) and the selection of a task that had the potential to help students achieve the goals (lines 12–16). Once he had determined what he was going to do and why, Nick turned his attention to anticipating what was likely to happen as students went to work on the task, and he endeavored to support their efforts. We now consider the three aspects of anticipating discussed at the beginning of the chapter and consider Mr. Bannister's engagement in each component of this practice.

Anticipating what students will do

Nick considered approaches that his students were likely to take, as shown in figure 4.2, and identified aspects of the task that might challenge them. For example, he hypothesized that some students might—

- have trouble finding the point of intersection in the table if the number of minutes increased by a number that wasn't a factor of 50 (lines 26–28);

- start the table at some number of minutes other than zero (lines 36–38);

- have notational difficulties (lines 43–44); or

- confuse what was fixed and what was changing (line 48–50).

What is clear is that Nick did more than just list approaches students might take (e.g., make a table, draw a graph, construct an equation)—he actually used the approach to solve the problem. By "getting inside the problem," Nick was able to consider the challenges that students might face and what he could do about them.

Although Nick may not have anticipated everything that his students might do, it is likely that he anticipated much of what would happen when they engaged in this task. His preparatory work would help him make sense of what he did see and free him up to consider more deeply the things that emerged that he had not anticipated.

Planning how to respond to student approaches

In addition to anticipating how students might solve the task, Nick also considered how he would respond to what students were doing. This was a critical component of his planning process because it gave him time outside of the classroom with its hectic pace to think about what actions he might take and the questions he might ask to move students toward the goals of the lesson without telling them what to do and how. Specifically, Nick considered how he would help students who created a table with 20-minute increments find the point of intersection (lines 28–36), who failed to include 0 minutes in their tables (lines 36–40), who struggled with writing four cents (lines 44–46), or who confused the fixed rate with the rate of change in the problem (lines 50–53).

Although Nick's list of questions that he might ask his students as they worked on the task was certainly not exhaustive, having some specific questions ready in advance of the lesson meant that Nick would not need to develop all the questions on the spot and gave him more time to consider when would be an appropriate moment to ask a particular question to help to make connections between what students were actually doing and the mathematics that he wanted them to learn. Because questions are bound to the context in which they are asked, it is critical to pose a question that makes a connection with issues that are currently being addressed. Developing questions only "in the moment" is very challenging for a teacher who is juggling the needs of a classroom full of learners who need different types and levels of assistance. When teachers feel overwhelmed by the needs and frustrations of their students, it is easy for them to revert to just telling students what to do when an alternative course of action does not immediately come to mind.

Identifying responses that address mathematical goals

After anticipating what his students might do and how he would respond to some of the approaches that they had taken, Nick determined that it would be important during the discussion to refer to a table, an equation, and a graph (lines 56–62) to achieve his goals for the lesson. Specifically, both the table and graph would help students in understanding that there was a point of intersection (goal 1); the graph would help students explore what happens to the functions before and after the point of intersection, and why (goal 2); and working with all three representations would allow students to make connections between and among them and to identify how the slope and y-intercept are manifested in each (goal 3).

To keep track of what students were actually doing during the lesson, Nick decided to make a chart (fig. 4.3). Such a chart serves as a record that can be used for a variety of purposes. By providing a record of who is doing what, the chart can help a teacher keep track of the approaches that are available in the classroom and can serve as a data source for making judgments about who will share what during the discussion. The chart can also be useful beyond the day of the lesson. It can help the teacher keep track of how students in the class are thinking about particular ideas and which students were selected to share their work with their peers on a particular day. It can also provide a historical record of what happened during the lesson that can aid the teacher in refining the lesson the next time it is taught.

Monitoring

Monitoring is the process of paying attention to the thinking of students during the actual lesson as they work individually or collectively on a particular task. This involves not just listening in on what students are saying and observing what they are doing, but also keeping track of the approaches that they are using, identifying those that can help advance the mathematical discussion later in the lesson, and asking questions that will help students make progress on the task. These questions might include those that will get students back on track if they are following an unproductive or inaccurate pathway, or that will press students who are on the right course to think more deeply about why things work the way that they do. We now return to the Case of Nick Bannister as he monitors his students' work in an effort to support their learning and engagement with the task and to prepare for the end-of-class discussion.

ACTIVE ENGAGEMENT 4.3

The second part of the Case of Nick Bannister focuses on the practice of monitoring. As you read part 2—

- identify specific things that Nick does to support his students' learning; and

- consider how the data that Nick collected in his chart (see fig. 4.4) could be useful to him as he helps students and prepares for the end-of-class discussion.

Calling Plans: The Case of Nick Bannister (Part 2—Monitoring)

After introducing the task to students and making sure that they understood what they needed to do, Nick Bannister set students to work on the task in their groups of four. He had decided to have each group create a poster that included the stu-
75 dents' answer to the question (i.e., How much time per month would you have to talk on the phone before subscribing to company A would save you money?) as well as all the work that they did to arrive at the answer. Because they could be displayed side by side, the posters would make it easier to look across different solutions and representations during the whole-class discussion and facilitate comparisons among different approaches.
80

    Armed with his monitoring tool—the chart shown in figure 4.3—Mr. Bannister listened in on the small-group conversations. He asked questions as needed to get students on the right track or to press them to make sense of what they were doing while he kept track of who was doing what. For example, when
85 Nick approached group 2, he noticed that the students had made a table that started at zero minutes and then increased by 10-minute intervals up to 60 minutes. (In fact, he thought their table looked like his (see table A in fig. 4.2). When he asked the students what they learned from the table, they responded that plans A and B cost the same for 50 minutes. He reminded them that they needed to figure out
90 when subscribing to company A would be able to save money and asked them how the table would help them. After a few seconds of silence, Camilla responded that if they were the same at 50 minutes, then at 51 minutes, plan A would be $7.04

and plan B would be $7.10, and that A would never again catch up to B. Nick then asked the group if they could just sketch what they thought the graph would look like without plotting all the points.

By contrast, when Nick approached group 6, he saw that the students had used the erroneous equation ($C = .4m + 5$) to create a table of values that showed the cost for increments of 5 minutes. The costs, of course, were much higher than they should have been. This was a notational error that Nick had anticipated, so he engaged the group in a conversation that he hoped would help them see and correct the problem.

Mr. Bannister:	Tell me what everything in the equation means.
Derrick:	Like, say, we want to figure out for 30 minutes for company A. I put, I put 30 minutes times .4, plus $5.00.
Mr. Bannister:	OK, and what did you get?
Derrick:	And I got $17.00.
Mr. Bannister:	All right.
Tanya:	So 4 represents cents per minute.
Mr. Bannister:	OK.
Tanya:	So, like every minute is 4 cents. So we kept, like, adding the 4 cents plus 5, 'cause that's like the fee, like the starting point.
Mr. Bannister:	OK. I understand what you are saying. The only thing I'm a little confused about is how do you write four cents in money?
Derrick:	.4.
Tanya:	Yeah.
Latasha:	.04.
Mr. Bannister:	Is it .4 or .04? Because it's a big difference there. When you write four cents in money, how would you write it? Say you wanted to write five dollars and four cents. What would you write?
William:	5.04.
Mr. Bannister:	So when you put 4 cents into the calculator. What did you put?
Derrick:	.4.
Mr. Bannister:	And what should you have put?
Latasha:	.04.
Mr. Bannister:	OK. With .04, you're on the right track; you just need to fix the table. So you might have to change these a little bit [*pointing to the values in the table*]. OK? So try 30 minutes with .04, and tell me what you get.
Derrick:	$6.20. Oh [*noting that the initial cost that the group had recorded for 30 minutes was $17*].
Mr. Bannister:	OK, $6.20. Hmmm…

135   At this point, Nick left the group, and the students continued to adjust the values in their table to reflect the change in their equation from C = .4*m* + 5 to C= .04*m* + 5.

Although Nick had anticipated much of what had occurred, the students did four things that he hadn't considered. First, group 1 started out by using 1 minute
140   as the increment for their table. By the time Nick got to the group, they were up to 15 minutes and were becoming convinced that the cost of plan B would never catch up to that of plan A (in other words, B would always be a better deal than A). He found that a few simple questions—"Do you need to go up by 1?" "Do you talk on the phone only 1 minute at a time?"—motivated students to consider
145   alternatives, finally leading them to decide to use 20-minute intervals.

Second, group 4 produced an accurate table using increments of 10 minutes but ended up graphing the number of minutes on the *y*-axis and the cost on *x*-axis. Nick started by telling the students that mathematicians customarily put the independent variable on the *x*-axis and the dependent variable on the *y*-axis, and
150   then he asked whether cost depends on the number of minutes, or the number of minutes depends on cost. Because this assignment of variables to axes is a convention and not open to discussion, he thought that he should first tell the students which variable goes where, but then let them decide which was which. After a short debate, the group members agreed that cost depended on the number of
155   minutes that someone talked on the phone. This led the students to create a new graph that showed the independent variable (number of minutes) on the *x*-axis and the dependent variable (cost) on the *y*-axis.

Third, group 3 (Devas, Andrea, Yolanda, and Chris) had trouble making progress on the task. When Nick approached the group and asked what they were
160   doing, they explained that they were trying to figure out how many minutes were in a month. Nick then engaged the students in the following exchange:

Mr. Bannister:	It could be any number of minutes, right? Can't you just use your phone any time you want?
Devas:	Yeah, but there's a certain amount. It depends, 'cause on different plans, you can have a certain amount of minutes.
Andrea:	Or like, you pay—if you passed a certain amount of minutes, you have to pay extra money—that's what we're trying to find out.
Mr. Bannister:	All right. The problem asks you just to say at what point would company A be a better deal than company B. How about if I talked on the plan from company A, let's say, just for one minute? You know how much it would cost if I talked, and I had company A? How much would….
Yolanda:	OK, $5.04.
Mr. Bannister:	Why would it be $5.04?
Yolanda:	Because it's 4 minutes per, it's 4 cents per minute.
Mr. Bannister:	OK. And what if I talked for 2 minutes on the plan from company A?
Chris:	Uh, $5.08.

180	Mr. Bannister:	OK. Now let me talk on the plan from company B for a minute—what if I talked for 1 minute, and I had my cell phone through company B?
	Devas:	Easy—$2.10.
	Mr. Bannister:	OK, $2.10. How about if I talked for 2 minutes?
185	Andrea:	Well, … $2.20.
	Mr. Bannister:	Good—$2.20. So which one that we've talked about so far is the better deal? Would you rather go with company A or company B?
	Chris:	Company B.
190	Mr. Bannister:	But the question asks you when is company A going to be the better deal?
	Yolanda:	So it's going to be after the intersection. Right?
	Chris:	If there is an intersection.
195	Devas:	They're probably going to intersect at the time point—like if we do a graph, we'll probably see them intersect.

At that point, Nick told the group that they were on the right track and that now they had to figure out if there was a point of intersection, and if so, what it would be and how finding it would help them answer the question. His experience with group 3 made him realize that the phone plans that students

200 actually had were much more complicated than the two that he had given them to work on and that perhaps their real-world knowledge was in fact getting in the way rather than helping them. He decided to make note of this so that he could think about how to set up the task in the future in a way that would avoid such problems.

205 Fourth, as students were finishing up their posters, Nick noticed that groups 4 and 6 had indicated that plan A became cheaper at 50 minutes rather than at 51 minutes, and he noted this on his monitoring chart. Although he had discussed this explicitly with group 2, he had not specifically asked other groups about it. He was not concerned, however, and thought a discussion of

210 what the answer should be and why would be a good way to launch the lesson.

At the end of 30 minutes, Nick had completed the monitoring chart, as shown in figure 4.4. He was pleased to see that groups used a combination of tables, graphs, and equations and that with the exception of the four things previously discussed, he had done a good job in anticipating what would occur.

215 Armed with the data that he had collected, Nick felt that he was now able to determine which solutions he wanted to focus on during the discussion.

Analysis of Monitoring in the Case of Nick Bannister

In part 2 of the Case of Nick Bannister, we see a teacher who paid careful attention to what his students were doing during the lesson in an effort to document what they had done, support them in their work, and plan for a productive closing discussion. So what did Nick actually do? First,

Strategy	Who and What	Order
Table	Group 1 started with increments of 1 but then gave it up and used increments of 20 Groups 2, 3, and 4 used increments of 10	
Graph	Group 1 used a calculator to create a graph from their table Group 2 made a sketch of a graph but did not plot the points Groups 3 and 4 each made a graph from their table	
Equation	Group 5 made an equation and then created a graph by using 0 minutes and 100 minutes Group 6 started with the equation and used it to create a table of values incremented by 5	
Other	Group 3 had trouble understanding the context of the problem Group 4 confused the axes on their initial graph Group 6 was confused about notation and initially had used .4 instead of .04	

Group 1: Tamika, Nina, Harold, Kisha
Group 2: Camilla, Jason, Lynette, Robert
Group 3: Devas, Andrea, Yolanda, Chris
Group 4: Mary, Jessica, Richard, Colin (50 minutes)
Group 5: James, Tony, Christine, Melissa
Group 6: Latasha, Derrick, Tanya, William (50 minutes)

Fig. 4.4. Nick Bannister's completed chart for monitoring students' work on the Calling Plans task

he collected data about what each group did, highlighting which representations the students used and any initial difficulties that they may have experienced, as shown in figure 4.4. The data made salient both the similarities among groups in the representations that they used in solving the task (e.g., five of the six groups created tables, five of the six groups made graphs) and the differences in how they created the representations (e.g., group 1 used calculators to create a graph from their table; group 2 made a sketch of the graph but did not plot the points; group 5 created a graph by using 0 minutes and 100 minutes in their equation). These data paint a vivid picture of "where the class is" and will help Nick in determining which solutions to share and in what order (the next two practices). As Lampert (2001, p. 140) summarizes, "If I watch and listen during small group independent work, I am then able to use my observations to decide *what* and *who* to make focal" during whole-class discussion.

Second, Nick took an active role in supporting students in making progress toward the lesson goals by helping those who were experiencing difficulty get back on track (e.g., group 6, lines 96–134; group 4, lines 146–57; group 3, lines 158–98). At the same time, he pressed students who were on a correct pathway to think more deeply about what they were doing and what it meant (e.g., group 2, lines 84–91; group 1, lines 139–45). The actions of Nick Bannister stand in sharp contrast with those of David Crane, whom we met in the Leaves and Caterpillars vignette in the introduction. Whereas Mr. Crane observed what students did but did little to understand the source of their confusion or the nature of their thinking, Nick Bannister, by questioning students in the way that he did, learned a great deal about his students' thinking. This information will help him in planning subsequent instruction, including, but not limited to, the discussion at the end of the lesson.

Conclusion

Anticipating and monitoring are crucial steps for teachers who want to make productive use of students' thinking during a lesson. By first anticipating the wide range of things that a student might do (and identifying which of those might be mathematically useful in achieving the lesson's goals), a teacher is in a better position to recognize and understand what students actually do. Teachers who have engaged in this kind of anticipation and prediction can then use their understanding of student work to make instructional decisions that will advance the mathematical understanding of the class as a whole. Although a teacher can't anticipate everything that might occur in the classroom when a particular group of students engages with a specific task, whatever the teacher can predict in advance of the lesson will be helpful in making sense of students' thinking during the lesson. As we saw in the Case of Nick Bannister, because Nick had predicted much of what did occur, he was left with a limited number of "in the moment" decisions. But having taught the lesson once, Nick now has a better sense of how students will respond, and he will be in an even better position to support learning the next time he teaches it.

In the Case of Nick Bannister, we saw a teacher who, as a result of his anticipating and monitoring, is ready to orchestrate a discussion of the Calling Plans task that builds on students' thinking. In the next chapter, we continue our discussion of the five practices with a focus on selecting, sequencing, and connecting, and in doing so, we return to Nick Bannister's classroom to see how the whole-group discussion unfolds.

TRY THIS!

Select a high-level task that has the potential to help students achieve a learning goal that you have identified. Individually, or in collaboration with one or more colleagues, do the following:

- Anticipate all the ways in which students are likely to solve the task and the errors that they might make.
- Consider questions that you could ask about these approaches that could help students in making progress on the task.
- Create a monitoring sheet that you can use to record data during the lesson.

CHAPTER 5

Determining the Direction of the Discussion: Selecting, Sequencing, and Connecting Students' Responses

Once teachers have completed the work of monitoring—attending to what students are doing and saying as they work on a task, providing guidance as needed, and keeping track of who is doing what—they are ready to make decisions about the direction that the discussion will take. Central to the decision-making process is an awareness of the key mathematical ideas that they want their students to learn (as discussed in chapter 2) and what students currently know and understand related to those ideas (as reflected in the data collected by using the monitoring tool, as discussed in chapter 4). Teachers must then *select* which ideas and students to focus on to advance the mathematical understanding of the group, and they must *sequence* the solutions in such a way as to provide a coherent and compelling story line for the lesson. Finally, they must determine how they will *connect* these various approaches to one another and to the mathematical ideas that are at the heart of the lesson.

In this chapter, we return to the Case of Nick Bannister, now focusing on parts 3 and 4 to consider how Nick used the data that he collected during the monitoring phase of the lesson to make decisions regarding the selecting, sequencing, and connecting of student responses. In considering these three practices, we first discuss practices 3 and 4, selecting and sequencing, together and then turn our attention to practice 5, connecting. In each of our discussions, we begin by describing the practice or practices under consideration, then we present the relevant part of the Case of Nick Bannister, and then we analyze Nick Bannister's use of the practice or practices.

Selecting and Sequencing

Selecting is the process of determining which ideas (*what*) and students (*who*) the teacher will focus on during the discussion. This is a crucial decision, since it determines what ideas students will have the opportunity to grapple with and ultimately to learn. Selecting can be thought of as the act of purposefully determining what mathematics students will have access to—beyond what they were able to consider individually or in small groups—in building their mathematical understanding.

Selecting is critical because it gives the teacher control over what the whole class will discuss, ensuring that the mathematics that is at the heart of the lesson actually gets on the table. We have come to think of the question, "Who wants to present next?" as either the bravest or most naïve invitation that can be issued in the classroom. By asking for volunteers to present, teachers relinquish control over the conversation and leave themselves—and their students—at the mercy of the student whom they have placed at center stage. Although this may work out fine—what the student presents may be both understandable and connected to the lesson goal—unfiltered student contributions can be difficult to follow or can take the conversation in an unproductive direction.

For example, in a second-grade classroom that we observed several years ago, students were learning to count by twos and were trying to determine the number of hands that there would be in a room of 12 students. When the class reconvened after a period of small-group exploration, the teacher asked various students what they had gotten as an answer and how they had gotten it. After two students had volunteered to share their solution (24) and their correct thinking about how they found it, the teacher asked for another volunteer to share. This student indicated that he got 23 hands. The teacher clearly did not expect this. Although she proceeded to ask the student a number of questions, she was unable to understand his reasoning or to pinpoint where it had gone wrong. The student unwittingly broke the flow of the discussion, leaving the class and the teacher puzzled. Although the teacher needed to explore and correct the thinking that had led to this solution, doing so in front of the whole class without any advance thought was not productive. Instead, she might have talked with the student privately at the end of the class or prior to the next class.

Although selecting is first and foremost about *what* mathematics will be highlighted, it is also about *who* will do it. For example, in Mr. Crane's class, two students (Janine and Kyra) used a unit rate strategy to solve the Leaves and Caterpillar task, as shown in figure 0.2. If Mr. Crane determines that this is a powerful strategy that he wants his students to understand (the *what*), he then needs to determine which student he will ask to do so (the *who*). In making this decision, he may want to consider which student has not presented recently and give that student an opportunity to take center stage in the classroom. By so doing, the teacher can make sure that *all* students have the opportunity to be seen as authors of mathematical ideas and to demonstrate their competence. A periodic review of completed monitoring sheets collected from previous lessons would provide a record of which students had shared their work in the recent past.

Sequencing is the process of determining the order in which the students will present their solutions. The key is to order the work in such as way as to make the mathematics accessible to all students and to build a mathematically coherent story line. For example, if Devon, a student who was working on the Tiling a Patio task in Darcy Dunn's class, had presented his solution (see fig. 3.4) first instead of last, it might have been challenging for students to understand, since his approach—unlike any of the others—focused on subtracting the black tiles (representing the central garden) that weren't included in the border instead of summing only the tiles that were in the border. Instead, Ms. Dunn selected Beth to go first because her strategy was one that had been used by several students and would therefore, the teacher reasoned, be more accessible to the group.

Although having the most commonly used strategy presented first is one approach to sequencing solutions, it may not always be the best way to proceed. For example, if a misconception surfaces during work on a task, the teacher may want to begin the discussion by addressing this issue directly. In fact, in a task such as the Pizza Comparison, shown in figure 5.1, the incorrect solutions might be particularly important to discuss, since the main purpose of this task is to help students understand that the size of the portion represented by a fraction depends on the size of the whole from which the portion is taken. Therefore, it would be critical for students to discuss solution 4 and understand why this solution is not correct. Similarly, in Mr. Crane's class, discussing Missy and Kate's solution to the Leaves and Caterpillar task (see fig. 0.1) first would have provided an opportunity for the entire class to discuss why adding 10 does not preserve the relationship between leaves and caterpillars—a common misconception.

The Pizza Comparison Task

Goal	To help students understand that a fraction tells us only about the relationship between the part and the whole, not about the size of the whole or the size of the parts. (Adapted from Van de Walle [2004, p. 254].)
Task	Think carefully about the following question. Write a complete answer. You may use drawings, words, or numbers to explain your answer. Be sure to show all your work. Jose ate ½ of a pizza. Ella ate ½ of another pizza. Jose said that he ate more pizza than Ella, but Ella said they both ate the same amount. Use words and pictures to show that Jose could be right.

Jose is right 1	Jose is right 2	Jose is right 3	Jose is wrong 4	Jose is wrong 5
Jose's pizza is bigger than Ella's (Picture)	Jose's pizza is bigger than Ella's (Words)	Jose's pizza is bigger than Ella's (Words + Picture)	½ always equals ½	Jose and Ella shared the pizza
	Jose could be right because the pizza that Jose ate could have been bigger than the pizza that Ella ate.	*Jose could be right because his pizza could be bigger than Ella's.*	*They ate the same amount because both had ½.*	

Fig. 5.1. Goals and possible solutions for the Pizza Comparison task

Another alternative is for the teacher to have students present strategies that move from concrete to abstract. Consider the following task: Explain why the sum of any two odd numbers is always even (a version of this task is shown in fig. 2.2). In presenting solutions to this task, the teacher might want to begin with a concrete representation of odd and even numbers (fig. 5.2a), move to a more logical argument in narrative form (fig. 5.2b), and end with an algebraic proof (fig. 5.2c). This sequence would bring all students into the discussion, since the concrete representation would be accessible to everyone, and each successive strategy could be carefully tied to those that came before it so that students could ultimately see how the algebraic solution is related to the less abstract approaches.

a. Concrete model	**b. Logical argument**	**c. Algebraic proof**
If I take the numbers 5 and 11 and organize the counters as shown, you can see the pattern. 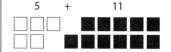 You can see that when you put the sets together (add the numbers), the two extra blocks will form a pair, and the answer is always even. This is because any odd number will have an extra block, and the two extra blocks for any set of two odd numbers will always form a pair. 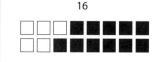	An odd number = [an] even number + 1; e.g., 9 = 8 + 1. So when you add two odd numbers you are adding an even number + an even number + 1 + 1. So you get an even number. This is because it has already been proved that an even number + an even number = an even number. Therefore, since an odd number = an even number + 1, if you add two of them together, you get an even number + 2, which is still an even number.	If a and b are odd integers, then a and b can be written $a = 2m + 1$ and $b = 2n + 1$, where m and n are other integers. If $a = 2m + 1$ and $b = 2n + 1$, then $a + b = 2m + 2n + 2$. If $a + b = 2m + 2n + 2$, then $a + b = 2(m + n + 1)$. If $a + b = 2(m + n + 1)$, then $a + b$ is an even integer.

Fig. 5.2. Possible solutions to the Odd + Odd = Even task

We now return to the Case of Nick Bannister, picking up this time where Nick is in the process of planning the *what* and the *who* for his students' whole-class discussion of the Calling Plans task.

ACTIVE ENGAGEMENT 5.1

- Review Nick Bannister's completed sheet for monitoring his students' work, as shown in figure 4.4.

- Given Mr. Bannister's goals for the lesson (see The Case of Nick Bannister—Part 1 in chapter 4, lines 3–11), determine which solutions (or parts of solutions) you would want to have students share, and in what order, during the discussion portion of the lesson, to accomplish the stated goals.

Calling Plans: The Case of Nick Bannister
(Part 3—Selecting and Sequencing)

Armed with the data that he had collected while he monitored his students' work, Nick was now ready to make decisions about the discussion. He knew from the out-set of the lesson that he would need to have a table, graph, and equation available to meet his lesson goals (lines 3–11 in part 1), so the real questions were, which table, graph, and equation, and in what order should they be presented? As Nick now in-dicated in the third column of the chart that he had used in monitoring his students (shown in fig. 5.3), he decided to start with the tables that had been created by groups 3 and 1, move to the sketch of the graph that had been created by group 2, and conclude with the equation that had been produced by group 5.

Strategy	Who and What	Order
Table	Group 1 started with increments of 1 but then gave it up and used 20 Groups 2, 3, and 4 used increments of 10	2nd (Tamika) 1st (Devas)
Graph	Group 1 used their calculator to create a graph from their table Group 2 made a sketch of a graph but did not plot the points Group 3 and 4 each made a graph from their table	3rd (Lynette)
Equation	Group 5 made an equation and then created a graph by using 0 minutes and 100 minutes Group 6 started with the equation and used it to create a table of values incremented by 5	4th (Tony)
Other	Group 3 had trouble understanding the context of the problem Group 4 confused the axes in their initial graph Group 6 was confused about notation and initially used 4 in-stead of .04	

Group 1: Tamika, Nina, Harold, Kisha
Group 2: Camilla, Jason, Lynette, Robert
Group 3: Devas, Andrea, Yolanda, Chris
Group 4: Mary, Jessica, Richard, Colin (50 minutes)
Group 5: James, Tony, Christine, Melissa
Group 6: Latasha, Derrick, Tanya, William (50 minutes)

Fig. 5.3. Nick Bannister's completed chart for monitoring students' work on the Calling Plans task

Nick decided to start the discussion by exploring whether the answer to the question, "How much time per month would you have to talk on the phone before subscribing to company A would save you money?" was 50 minutes or 51 minutes, since two groups thought the answer was 50 minutes (incorrect) and four groups thought the answer was 51 minutes (correct). He then planned to move to a discus-sion of tables because five of the six groups made a table, so it was the most com-monly used representation. He decided to discuss a table that was incremented by 10 minutes, because using 10-minute intervals was a popular approach and the resulting table clearly showed the point of intersection, as well as a table incremented by 20 minutes, because such a table did not show the point of intersection. This, he hoped, would launch a discussion about what we do or do not know about the functions from the table and what else we might need to do to answer the question.

240   Although several groups plotted points and connected them to make graphs, Nick decided to focus on the sketch of the graph created by group 2. And rather than have the group members explain what they had done and why, he decided that he would ask the class how group 2 knew what the graph was going to look like. This would focus students' attention on the question of how the table provides many "clues" about the graph and stimulate their thinking about how func-

245   tions behave (i.e., the functions have to be linear because they have a constant rate of change, they must have a point of intersection because they share a common point, and they start on the y-axis, which represents the monthly fee). By having the class consider this question, rather than listening to what group 2 did, Nick could engage more students in thinking about how they could figure it out. He

250   then thought he would check with group 2 and see whether what the other students described captured what they actually did.

He decided to end with the equation produced by group 5, since it was one of only two groups that produced the equation and the only group that did not create a table of values. He wanted the class to consider why the group members

255   used only two points in creating their graphs and whether or not this approach was valid. He also wanted students in the class to consider how the slope and y-intercept, which were key features of the equation, were salient in the tables and the graph.

Once Nick had decided which groups would present, he needed to figure out

260   which student would speak on behalf of each group. Although he sometimes had the entire group make the presentation, this strategy often resulted in one student doing most of the talking and the others receding to the background. He reviewed the membership of the groups he had targeted and identified presenters who had not had a chance to share their work in the last week (shown in column 3 of his

265   chart in fig. 5.3). The groups assumed that any member could be asked to present, so every student in the group needed to understand the work that the group had produced well enough to discuss it in front of the class. Nick found that this assumption on their part also helped him to hold all students accountable for participating in the small-group discussions.

Analysis of Selecting and Sequencing in the Case of Nick Bannister

In part 3 of the case, we see a teacher who thoughtfully considered how to use the work produced by his students as a basis for a whole-class discussion. He wanted to discuss the meaning of the point of intersection, the behavior of the functions before and after that point, and how the three representations of the functions (table, graph, and equation) provide insights into the situation and are connected to one another (see part 1 of the Case of Nick Bannister in chapter 4, lines 3–11). To accomplish this goal, Nick decided to have students present tables, a graph, and an equation (in that order), reflecting the frequency with which the representations were used in the class. He also identified key aspects of particular representations that would be fruitful points for discussion, such as how to find the point of intersection when it doesn't appear in the table (lines 234–36), how the behavior of a graph can be known without plotting specific points (lines 240–47), and how a graph can be created from an equation without generating a table of values (lines 252–54). By closely attending to students' work, he was able to uncover interesting features that would be likely to provoke the thinking of the entire class. Hence, he used his goals for the lesson and his knowledge of "where various students' thinking was" to guide his decisions regarding what ideas would be put on the table for the discussion and in what order.

In this lesson, Nick decided to begin by discussing the answer to the question that framed the students' investigation ("How much time per month would you have to talk on the phone before subscribing to company A would save you money?") because students were not in agreement about whether the plan from company A became a better deal at 50 or 51 minutes (lines 226–30). Resolving the answer to this question would give students the opportunity to air their thinking, to listen to the opposing arguments, and to defend or refine their positions. This work can help students develop their skills of argumentation and begin to assume some authority for determining what is and isn't correct.

It appears that Nick decided not to discuss in the public forum any of the difficulties that students had as they worked on this problem. He may have felt that the problems that students encountered were localized in particular groups, and through his interactions with the groups, he was able to help them move beyond the challenges that they were facing. Alternatively, he may have thought that although some of the issues were important and could have long-range consequences (e.g., group 4's confusion about which variable to graph on which axis), he did not wish to use class time during this lesson to address them. Given his limited time, he had to make decisions about how to spend his 50 minutes of instruction most effectively.

Although it is clear that Nick made thoughtful decisions about the best ways to highlight the mathematics to be learned, he was also making thoughtful decisions about his students (lines 259–65). He carefully considered the composition of each group and which students to ask to speak on behalf of the group. By selecting students who had not presented recently, he was giving them the opportunity to demonstrate their competence and to gain confidence in their abilities. His practice of identifying one member of the group to present was also a way to hold all members of the group accountable for the work of the group.

There are many ways different ways that student responses could be selected and sequenced that could be equally productive. The point is that the method selected must support the story line that the teacher envisions for the lesson so that the mathematics to be learned emerges in a clear and explicit way. Nick's work suggests that he is well positioned to orchestrate such a discussion.

Connecting

Connecting may in fact be the most challenging of all of the five practices because it calls on the teacher to craft questions that will make the mathematics visible and understandable. Hence, the questions must go beyond merely clarifying and probing what individual students did and how. Instead, they must focus on mathematical meaning and relationships and make links between mathematical ideas and representations. Boaler and Humphries (2005, p. 38) argue that such questions "serve a very particular and deliberate purpose: challenging students to consider a critical mathematical concept."

Although questions need to expose the mathematics to be learned in an explicit way, they must begin with what students know. Moving between where a child is and where one ultimately wants him or her to end up mathematically "is a continuous reconstruction," (Dewey 1902, p. 11). In this same vein, Ball (1993, p. 394) argues, "I must consider the mathematics in relation to the children and the children in relation to the mathematics," suggesting the teacher's need to know both the mathematics to be learned and what students know about mathematics to bridge the two worlds. To consider one without considering the other can result in questions that draw blank stares because they make no connection with students' current ways of thinking. To consider one without the other can also result in students' thinking remaining stagnant, instead of moving toward new mathematical understandings. For this reason, framing questions in the context of students' work is critical.

Consider, for example, the questions that a teacher may wish to ask about the Odd + Odd = Even task (task B in fig. 2.2). Imagine that the teacher's goal for the lesson built around this task is for students to recognize that (1) proofs must be general arguments that apply to all cases, and (2) algebra can be used to represent a general argument. In a discussion of the solutions to this task (shown in fig. 5.2), the teacher might want to ask students to determine whether each of the solutions is in fact a proof, to explain why or why not, and to show how each representation is connected with the others. Through this discussion, students could come to see that the "extra block" in the representation of an odd number in the concrete model is the same as the +1 in the logical argument and in the algebraic proof, and that the even number described in the logical argument is represented by a 2-by-something rectangle in the concrete model and by $2n$ in the algebraic proof. The discussion could make salient the idea that $2n$ can be represented as a rectangle that has the dimensions of 2 and n and that this fact is related to what it means to be *even*—an even number is divisible by 2—so that any even number can be made into a rectangle with two rows. Without specific questions that make the connections between the different strategies, highlight how each addresses evenness and oddness, and make explicit how each meets the criteria for proof, the lesson would become a show-and-tell, and the link to key ideas in the discipline (e.g., proofs are logical arguments that show that conjectures are always true; proofs can be expressed symbolically, pictorially, or in narrative form) would be lost. It is the questions and their close connection to the context—the actual solutions produced by students—that can advance students' understanding of mathematics.

The key to connecting is to make sure that the mathematics to be learned is openly addressed. Consider the Pizza Comparison task (see fig. 5.1). In a discussion of solutions 3, 4, and 5, it would be important to elicit arguments regarding which is correct, and why, and to explicitly address (1) whether portions that are ½ (or any fractional amount) always represent the same size, and (2) what determines how big a ½ portion actually is. The teacher in this situation might want to ask students to create situations where the same fraction clearly refers to different-sized pieces to ensure that students have a solid understanding of this important idea. In looking across the three solutions, students might also be asked how they are the same and how they are different. Their responses to this question would highlight the fact that each solution correctly portrays the fraction ½, but the wholes from which the halves are taken are different.

An important consideration related to facilitating the actual discussion is considering how the students will share the work. For example, Mr. Bannister asked his students to create posters of their work because he thought that it would be easier to look across different representations during the whole-class discussion (lines 74–80). (It is worth noting that the expense of chart paper may limit its use; in addition, making posters can turn mathematical activities into time-consuming art projects, and posters will be less effective if all the work is likely to be similar.) Ms. Dunn had prepared transparencies that contained the first three figures in the pattern sequence so that students could simply describe and show what they had done without having to draw the patios. Although the use of transparencies makes it somewhat more challenging to compare strategies because only one transparency can be displayed at a time, a list of the generalizations, along with the names of the students who created them, on the board or chart paper (see Darcy Dunn's list in fig. 3.5) can enable students to keep track of the full range of ideas that are on the table. Alternatively, document projectors that allow students to display their original work without having to recopy it on a poster or transparency may be most efficient. With the document camera, it is possible to show more than one solution by using the zoom to make the images smaller.

We now return to the Case of Nick Bannister to see how Nick helps his students make connections during the discussion.

ACTIVE ENGAGEMENT 5.2

- Review Nick Bannister's completed monitoring chart shown in figure 5.3.

- Given Nick's goals for the lesson (see The Case of Nick Bannister—Part 1 in chapter 4, lines 2-11), identify questions that you would want to ask students about the representations to achieve these goals.

Calling Plans: The Case of Nick Bannister (Part 4—Connecting)

270   Nick started the final phase of his lesson (sharing and summarizing) by placing the six posters across the whiteboard in the front of the room in the following sequence: group 3, group 1, group 2, group 5, group 4, and group 6. Although he didn't plan to discuss the work of groups 4 and 6 formally, he thought that these groups might choose to make some connection between what other groups did

275   and what they had done.

        Before discussing the individual posters, Nick started the discussion by asking the class how much time someone would have to talk on the phone before subscribing to company A would save money. Students shouted out "50 minutes" and "51 minutes," both of which Nick recorded on the side board. He asked

280   if someone who thought it was 50 minutes would explain his or her thinking. When recognized by the teacher, Jessica said, "Both plans cost $7.00 for 50 minutes, so that is when A starts getting better." Nick asked if anyone wanted to add anything to what Jessica had said. Colin said, "That's where the two lines cross on our graph, so it has to be 50." Yolanda was waving her hand wildly, and when

285   Nick acknowledged her, she blurted out, "But 50 is where they are the same, so you have to go one more."

Nick thought that Yolanda's comment provided a good transition to looking at the posters, and he asked Devas to come up and explain how his group had used the table (group 3's table in fig. 5.4) that they had created to arrive at an answer of 51 minutes. Devas explained, "They are the same for 50 minutes, but when you go to 60, we saw that plan A was cheaper than plan B for the first time, and that as we kept going, we could tell that A would never catch up to B. They are the same for 50, so we tried 51, and we got $7.04 for plan A and $7.10 for plan B. So we think the answer has to be 51, not 50." Nick asked if what Devas and Yolanda said made sense to the students who thought it was 50. Jessica said that she thought they were just supposed to find where they were the same, so she wanted to revise her answer. Nick asked if anyone had any questions, and after waiting about ten seconds for a response, he decided to move on.

Group 3

min.	cost A	cost B
0	5.00	2.00
10	5.40	3.00
20	5.80	4.00
30	6.20	5.00
40	6.60	6.00
50	7.00	7.00
60	7.40	8.00
70	7.80	9.00
80	8.20	10.00
90	8.60	11.00
100	9.00	12.00

Group 1

min.	cost A	cost B
0	5.00	2.00
20	5.80	4.00
40	6.60	6.00
60	7.40	8.00
80	8.20	10.00
100	9.00	11.00

Fig. 5.4. Tables produced by groups 3 and 1 for the Calling Plans task

Nick then asked Tamika if she could explain how the members of her group found the answer by using their table (group 1's table in fig. 5.4). She said that they decided to go by 20s because they started going by 1s, and it was taking forever. She explained, "We would have probably kept going past 100 because we didn't see anything happening, but Mr. B asked us to look at our numbers and see if we could find a place where A was more expensive than B and a place where A was less expensive than B. Then we saw that A was higher at 40 and lower at 60. But we weren't sure what it meant, so we got the graphing calculator and entered the table and made the graph. Then we could see that the lines crossed at 50 minutes—right in between 40 and 60." Nick asked Tamika what they thought this meant. She explained, "B was cheaper before 50 minutes, and A was cheaper after."

At this point, Nick decided to move on to the graph. He pointed to the sketch that group 2 had made (shown in fig. 5.5) and invited the class to consider what the group must have done in drawing the sketch. The following exchange ensued between Nick and his students:

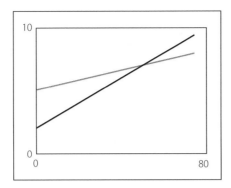

Fig. 5.5. Group 2's sketch of the graphs of the two phone plans

Mary:	I'm thinking that if you look at the table, you can see that they might figure out what the cost had gone up by, so it—and it's going by the same amount—so it must be linear, and since it had an intersection point, they made it cross.
Mr. Bannister:	What else helped them make this graph, this little sketch of it?
Richard:	What helped them, like, get company A and B—they started out with that 5 and 2.
Mr. Bannister:	OK. So company A and B start off at $5 and $2, and how did they show that on the graph?
Richard:	'Cause where it said 0, they just moved up like 2 spaces and 5 spaces.
Mr. Bannister:	What does that mean?
Richard:	If you don't talk any minutes at all, you still have to pay the fee.
Mr. Bannister:	OK, so which one would you say is company B, based on what you're telling me? Because they didn't label them. Come up and show me.
Melissa:	This one right here [*pointing to the darker line in fig. 5.5*].
Mr. Bannister:	OK, and why would you pick that line for company B?
Melissa:	Because company B starts off at 2 and that's where they draw it—at 2.
Mr. Bannister:	OK [*addressing group 2, whose members drew the graph*], is that something that you did when you sketched your graph?
[*Students in group 2 agree, with some saying, "Yeah."*]	
Mr. Bannister:	OK. I just want to go back to one more thing about this graph. Mary said that she knew it was linear by looking at the table. Can you explain more to me about that?
Mary:	I figured out from the table, company A and company B, like how much they're going by…
Mr. Bannister:	Yes…
Mary:	Yeah, and they're going by the same amount, so that's why I'm thinking that it's linear.
Mr. Bannister:	OK. Does anyone want to add to that?

315

320

325

330

335

340

James:		I know what she means because you can tell that in the table. It keeps going up by the same amount and never changes. Like for company A, it keeps going up 4 cents—4 cents for every minute.
345		
Colin:		It's a pattern.
James:		That's why the graph is a line.
Mr. Bannister:		But does it go up by 4 cents in the table? I am not seeing that.
Tamika:		Well, our table goes up by 80 cents for 20 minutes, but that is the same as 4 cents per minute. That's what we had when we first started, but then we changed.
Mr. Bannister:		OK, so does that mean that if something goes up by the same amount, it's going be linear every time?

[*Students give general assent, with many saying, "Yeah."*]

Mr. Bannister:		OK. Who can tell me by looking at the equation [*pointing to the equation on group 4's poster: C = .04m + 5*] whether we know how it's going to be linear or not? Yes?
Tony:		'Cause it's always multiplying by the same thing.
Mr. Bannister:		Always multiplying by the same thing. What is being multiplied by the same thing?
Tony:		For every minute that you put in for *m*, you multiply by the cost of 4 cents per minute.

Nick then asked the class what the point of intersection means in the problem. Yolanda volunteered that the point of intersection is where the two lines cross. Nick agreed but asked her what it means in terms of the problem. Yolanda explained that it is where the plans cost the same. Nick pointed to zero minutes for plan A and 30 minutes for plan B (see group 3's table in fig. 5.4) and asked the class, "Didn't they cost the same here too?" Yolanda responded, "Yeah, they do. But not for the same number of minutes. Where they intersect, both the minutes and the cost are the same."

At this point, Nick indicated that he wanted to return to a point that Tamika had raised earlier. He reminded the class that she had said that B was cheaper before 50 minutes, and A was cheaper after. He asked students to turn to the person next to them and talk for 2 minutes about whether they agreed or disagreed with this statement, and why. A quick polling of the groups indicated that all of the groups agreed with what Tamika had said, but most were not sure how to explain their thinking. William volunteered to try. He began, "We think it has something to do with the fact that the one with the higher fee costs less per minute." Colin jumped in: "So the one with the higher fee costs more if you only talk a little bit, but if you talk more, it eventually gets cheaper. Like the fee gets spread out over more minutes." Nick asked Lynette if this could be seen on the sketch of the graph. She responded, "Well, you can see that plan A starts at 5 and goes up, and plan B starts at 2 and goes up. But B is steeper than A, so it goes up faster." Nick asked, "Why does it go up faster?" Lynette said that it goes up faster because the

385   cost per minute is more. Nick summarized, "So Colin and Lynette are pointing out that although plan A costs more than plan B for zero minutes, since it costs less per minute than plan B, it will at some point cost less. And we already found out that that point is 51 minutes. Does anyone have any questions?" Latasha asked, "So are you saying that no matter what the fee is, that the plan with the

390   cheaper minutes will be better?" Nick acknowledged that this was a great question and wrote it on the side board.

Nick told the class, "For homework tonight, I want you to answer Latasha's question and provide some examples of plans to support your position." He gave them a few minutes to write the question in their notebooks. Although he had

395   been planning to have students create new phone plans for homework (e.g., a plan that was always cheaper than both plans A and B; a plan that was always more expensive than plans A and B), he thought that the ideas that he wanted students to grapple with would come out of addressing Latasha's question.

Nick then asked Tony to explain how group 5 created its equations (for plan

400   A, $c = .04m + 5$, and for plan B, $c = .10m + 2$). Tony explained, "Well, we knew that every minute was 4 cents for plan A and 10 cents for plan B, so we needed to multiply them by the number of minutes (m), and then add on the monthly fee, because that doesn't change." Because only two groups wrote equations, Nick wanted to make sure that the other students understood what Tony was describ-

405   ing. Nick asked students in groups 1, 2, 3, and 4, who had started with tables and had not developed equations at all, what they thought about what Tony was saying. Devas said, "Well, that's what we did to make our table—we just didn't write it out like that, but it makes sense." Chris added, "I think I get it, as long as I know what c and m are supposed to be."

410   Nick then asked the class to focus on the equation for plan A and to explain where .04 and 5 would be in the graph and the table. Tamika explained, "It is like I said before. It is the amount that the table goes up. In our table, it goes up 80 cents each time, but that is for 20 minutes, so it is the same as 4 cents per minute. When we started our table, we had 1 minute was $5.04, and two minutes

415   was $5.08, so you could see the 4 cents better." Nick asked the students in group 3 where the 4 cents is in their table (see fig. 5.4). Yolanda said that the cost increased 40 cents for 10 minutes, so that was the same at 4 cents for 1 minute or 80 cents for 20 minutes.

Nick said, "What about the $5?" Almost immediately "zero minutes" was

420   being muttered by several students. Nick said, "I am hearing zero minutes. Does someone want to explain that?" Nick called on Christine, who had been very quiet. She commented, "Zero minutes costs $5. You can see it in all of the tables up there, and it is where line hits the y-axis on the graph." Nick saw a room full of nodding heads, which he took as agreement.

425   Class was nearly over, and Nick had one last question before the students finished. He pointed to the graph that group 5 had drawn (shown in fig. 5.6) and asked the class how this group—Tony's group—could have come up with the graph without making a table.

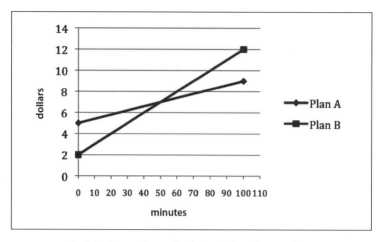

Fig. 5.6. Group 5's graph of the Calling Plans task

Kisha said, "Well, like they knew where the lines had to start, because their
430   equations had +5 and +2. I just don't see how they got the other point." Nick
asked Tony to explain where his group had gotten the other two points (100, 9)
for plan A and (100, 12) for plan B. Tony said, "Well we knew we needed two
points to have a line, and we only had one. So we just picked 100. So we put
100 in our equation and got the other number." Kisha asked, "Why did you
435   pick 100?" Tony replied, "It was James's idea, really." James jumped in, "Well, it
seemed like it would be easy to multiply. We could have picked anything." Nick
asked, "What if James had picked 40 instead of 100? Would it have mattered?
Melissa offered, "We would have still have had two lines, but they wouldn't have
crossed yet. So we could have just extended them."
440   At this point, only a minute was left in the class. Nick thanked the class for
a good discussion, reminded them about the homework, and told them that they
could use the last minute to start thinking about how they wanted to answer
Lastasha's question.

Analysis of Connecting in the Case of Nick Bannister

Nick Bannister's intent in this lesson was for his students to (1) recognize that there is a point of
intersection between two unique, nonparallel linear equations, representing where the two functions have the same x- and y-values; (2) understand that the two functions "switch positions" at the
point of intersection and that the one that was on "top" before the point of intersection is on the
"bottom" after the point of intersection because the function with the smaller rate of change will
ultimately be the function closer to the x-axis; and (3) make connections among tables, graphs, and
equations and be able to identify the slope and y-intercept in each representation. Through his work
with anticipating, monitoring, selecting, and sequencing, Nick had positioned himself to make
connections among different strategies used by students and with the mathematical ideas that were
central to the lesson.

Although it is clear that Nick's students were able to produce tables, equations, and graphs that would allow them to answer the question that was posed in the Calling Plans task, this was not his primary goal. Rather, the question (i.e., when would subscribing to company A save money?) provided a vehicle for unearthing ideas related to the point of intersection, the slope and y-intercept, and the behavior of systems of linear equations. Central to Nick's lesson were the questions that he asked for the purpose of engaging his students in making sense of the situation and in seeing how different representations provide insights into the behavior of the functions. It is also valuable to examine how Nick helped students make important connections by making the mathematical ideas public and explicit.

Mathematical ideas: The meaning of the point of intersection

Nick's first goal was for students to recognize that the point of intersection is the place where the two functions have the same x- and y-values. Several students had made reference to the fact that both plans cost the same at 50 minutes (lines 281–82; 290) and that this is where the two lines cross (lines 283–84; 307). Mary actually used the word "intersection point" for the first time (lines 316–17) in describing how the table would provide insight into what the graph would look like. Although there may have been an implicit understanding of the point of intersection, Nick directly asked the class what the point of intersection means in the problem (lines 363–65). He then pressed Yolanda until she stated that it is the point where "*both* the minutes and the cost are the same" (lines 368–70). Hence, Nick helped Yolanda explicitly connect the idea that the two plans have the same x- and y-values at a point, that the two lines cross at the point of intersection, and what it means in the context of the problem.

Mathematical ideas: Functions switch positions at the point of intersection

Nick's second goal for the lesson was for students to understand that the two functions "switch positions" at the point of intersection. This idea first came up when Tamika was explaining how her group had determined when company A would be cheaper than company B: "B was cheaper before 50 minutes, and A was cheaper after" (lines 308–09). Although Nick did not immediately pick up on this, he returned to this idea later and asked students to discuss whether they agreed or disagreed with Tamika's assertion, and why (lines 371–73). This led to the students' speculating that the phenomenon was related to the fact that the one with a higher fee cost less per minute (lines 377–78), that the one that starts out higher gets cheaper eventually (379–80), and that plan B is "steeper" than A, so it goes up faster (382–83). What was critical to this discussion was Nick's summary of the ideas that were currently on the table (lines 385–88): "So Colin and Lynette are pointing out that although plan A costs more than plan B for zero minutes, since it costs less per minute than plan B, it will at some point cost less. And we already found out that that point is 51 minutes. Does anyone have any questions?" Here Nick consolidated the ideas that had been presented into one clear and concise statement and turned it back to the students to consider. By leaving it open for additional exploration, he was inviting the students to continue to wrestle with the idea and see if they could make sense of it. This led to Latasha's question as to whether this idea could be generalized by stating that no matter what the fee is, the plan with the cheaper cost per minute will be better (lines 389–90). Nick acknowledged that this was an important question and decided to have students explore it for homework by creating plans that would test out the conjecture. In making this move, Nick acknowledged the importance of Latasha's contribution, built an opportunity for students to explore the idea independently so that he could see what sense they were making of it, and designed a homework assignment that aligned well with the lesson.

Mathematical ideas: Making connections among representations

Nick's third and final goal for the lesson was for students to make connections among tables, graphs, and equations and be able to identify the slope and y-intercept in each representation. Two key moves on his part made the connections salient. First, he invited students to consider how they could sketch a graph without plotting particular points (310–13). This exercise prompted students to consider how the table and the graph were connected. Students were able to discern that the constant rate of change in the tables (lines 314–16; 343–45) indicated that the functions would be linear, that a shared point indicated that the lines would intersect (lines 316–17), and that the value for zero minutes would be the y-intercept (lines 319–20; 323; 325). Although group 2 could have explained how they got their graph, it is unlikely that their explanation would have engaged the class in thinking about how information presented in one representational form offers insight into another.

The second move that Nick made that helped students to connect the representations was asking students to explain where .04 and 5 (in the equation for plan A) would be in the graph and in the table (lines 410–411). Here students talked about how 4 cents per minute is embedded in the tables because it is equivalent to 80 cents for 20 minutes (the increment in group 1's table in fig. 5.4) and to 40 cents for 10 minutes (the increment in group 3's table in the same figure). In addition, they discussed that $5 was the value for zero minutes in the tables and that it was the y-intercept on the graph (lines 422–24). One connection that Nick and his students do not seem to have made explicitly is where .04 would be on the graph. A specific question addressing this point might have led to a more explicit discussion of slope as the rate of change of the functions and how it plays out as "steepness" in the graphs.

In this particular task, making connections among different representations (a goal for the lesson) was directly related to making connections among the work presented by different students. For example, in having students comment on how they could have made a sketch of the graph without plotting points, students were making connections between the work that most of them had done in building tables and the work that group 2 had done in constructing its graph. In having students discuss where they would find .04 and 5 in different representational forms, students moved between the equations that group 5 had constructed and the tables and graphs that other groups had presented.

It is important to note that connections among solutions do not always arise naturally out of the discussion, as they seemed to do in this situation. Take for example the Odd + Odd = Even task that we have discussed previously. It is not clear that students would spontaneously see that each of the solutions (see fig. 5.2) deals with two critical ideas: that an odd number has an extra 1 that an even number does not have and that an even number is divisible by 2. Similarly, in Mr. Crane's class, it is unlikely that students would automatically see that the scale factor of 6 and the unit rate of 2.5 are central to each of the solutions. Highlighting these ideas by asking specific questions would serve to connect the different solutions with one another and with the mathematical ideas of the lesson.

Conclusion

Although anticipating and monitoring ensure that teachers have thought carefully about what students might do and say, and that they have paid close attention to students' thinking during the lesson, it is through selecting, sequencing, and connecting that teachers guarantee that key ideas are made public so that all students have the opportunity to make sense of mathematics. Although there are many ways to select, sequence, and connect responses, these decisions must be guided by what the teacher is trying to accomplish in the lesson. Hence, the goals for the lesson serve as a beacon toward which all activity is directed. As Hiebert and his colleagues (2007, p. 51) say, "Formulating clear, explicit learning goals sets the stage for everything else."

In the Case of Nick Bannister, we see a teacher who took this idea to heart. He clearly identified his goals early in the planning process and never lost sight of them as he moved through the actual implementation of the lesson. Although we might point to things about the lesson that could be improved, Nick's clear focus on what he wanted to accomplish led him to select, sequence, and connect the responses in such a way that the ideas with which he wanted students to grapple were in the public arena. Hatano and Inagaki (1991, p. 341) argue that "a group as a whole usually has a richer data base than any of its members for problem solving. It is likely that no individual member has acquired or has ready access to all needed pieces of information, but every piece is owned by at least one member in the group." Thus, during group discussion, all participants have the opportunity to "collect more pieces of information about the issue of the discussion and to understand the issue more deeply" (Hatano and Inagaki 1991, p. 346). Although Nick will need to do additional work to assess what individual students took away from the discussion, the homework that he assigned is likely to provide insights that will help him in designing subsequent instruction.

Our attention in chapters 4 and 5 has been on how to use the five practices to orchestrate a productive discussion. As a result of this targeted focus, we did not explicitly address other things that contribute to the success of the five practices. In the next chapter, we focus squarely on two aspects of orchestrating a discussion that deserve more focused attention: asking questions that focus on important ideas and holding students accountable for actively participating in the lesson.

TRY THIS!

- Teach the lesson you that planned at the conclusion of chapter 4. Collect data by using the monitoring sheet that you created and then indicate which solutions you will select and the order in which you will sequence the presentations.

- You may want to make an audio or video recording of the discussion so that you can reflect on the extent to which you were able to make connections among different solutions and with the mathematical ideas that were central to the lesson.

Ensuring Active Thinking and Participation: Asking Good Questions and Holding Students Accountable

The five practices can help teachers manage classroom discussions productively. However, they cannot stand alone. We have already discussed the importance of setting appropriate learning goals for students and selecting instructional tasks that provide students with opportunities to think and reason. In addition, teachers need to develop a range of ways of interacting with and engaging students as they work on tasks and share their thinking with other students. This includes having a repertoire of specific kinds of questions that can push students' thinking toward core mathematical ideas as well as methods for holding students accountable to rigorous, discipline-based norms for communicating their thinking and reasoning.

Why is the manner in which teachers interact with students so important as to warrant a separate chapter? *What* students learn is intertwined with *how* they learn it. And the stage is set for the *how* of learning by the nature of classroom-based interactions between and among teachers and students. Teachers might interact with students, and students with one another, in a variety of ways, ranging from abrupt, short-answer Q&A sessions to deeper explorations of mathematical concepts and ideas. Each of these styles of interaction is associated with different opportunities for student learning.

The purpose of this chapter is twofold: to help teachers develop good questioning skills that will challenge students to think at deeper levels, and to introduce teachers to a set of discussion "moves" that will help them to hold students accountable for their thinking and communication during classroom discussions. We begin by identifying and illustrating questions that can push students' thinking. After providing a short excerpt from Regina Quigley's fourth-grade classroom discussion, we analyze the different types of questions that the teacher asks. In the second part of this chapter, we introduce moves that teachers can use to promote the participation of students in whole-class discussions. A small number of accountable talk moves (Chapin, O'Connor, and Anderson 2003) will be introduced as strategies for encouraging accountability to the discipline, the community, and rigorous thinking.

Asking Good Questions

Perhaps the oldest and still most common form of teacher questioning is what is commonly referred to as the *IRE pattern,* in which the teacher *initiates* a question, the student *responds* (usually in one or two words), and the teacher *evaluates* the student's response as either right or wrong (Mehan 1979). IRE exchanges do little to deepen students' comprehension of the problem that is before them; rather, they teach students to guess the answer to the question that the teacher is looking for. Moreover, the authority for deciding if an answer is right or wrong lies solely with the teacher and not in discipline-based reasoning of any kind, leaving the student completely dependent on others for judging the veracity of his or her mathematical answers.

In the 1990s, as teachers began to see the value of having students construct their own approaches to solving cognitively rich problems, they began to turn away from the IRE pattern. Rather than tell students what to think and whether or not their answers were right or wrong, teachers wanted to foster students' development as active thinkers, constructors, and evaluators of knowledge. Unfortunately, most teachers were unprepared and did not know exactly how to do this. In addition, most students were unprepared for this style of interaction. Few students had had the opportunity to think hard about mathematical tasks; they were used to being shown the steps to use to solve a problem and then applying those steps to a set of similar problems. Even fewer students had been asked to represent or communicate their thinking; often their work was checked only for right or wrong answers, and their thinking typically remained invisible.

In what follows, we provide some concrete suggestions for ways in which teachers can induce students to think harder about cognitively challenging tasks. Good questions certainly help. They can guide students' attention to previously unnoticed features of a problem or they can loosen up their thinking so that they gain a new perspective on what is being asked. Good questions also force students to articulate their thinking so that it is understandable to another human being; this articulation, in and of itself, is often a catalyst to learning.

Figure 6.1 presents nine different types of questions used by teachers. Emerging from Boaler and Brodie's (2004) analysis of hundreds of mathematics lessons, these questions captured the full range of questions that teachers posed to students during observed instruction. What Boaler and Brodie found was that many teachers asked primarily questions of type 1, a finding that is consistent with the IRE pattern that we have discussed. However, classrooms in which teachers used a more diverse pattern of questioning led to higher student achievement.

Although Boaler and Brodie used these question types to document what was occurring in mathematics classrooms, they can also be useful to teachers who are trying to ask questions that go beyond gathering information or leading students through a procedure. We have highlighted three types of questions (rows 3, 4, and 5) that might be particularly important to ask, since they seek to highlight important ideas and relationships (type 3), probe students' thinking (type 4), and generate discussion among students (type 5).

Equally important is what these questions *do not do.* These questions *do not* take over the thinking for the students by providing too much information or by "giving away" the answer or a quick route to the answer. Rather, they scaffold thinking to enable students to think harder and more deeply about the ideas at hand.

	Question Type	Description
1	Gathering information, leading students through a procedure	Requires immediate answer. Rehearses known facts/procedures. Enables students to state facts/procedures.
2	Inserting technology	Once ideas are under discussion, enables correct mathematical language to be used to talk about them.
3	Exploring mathematical meanings and/or relationships	Points to underlying mathematical relationships and meanings. Makes links between mathematical ideas and representations.
4	Probing, getting students to explain their thinking	Asks student to articulate, elaborate, or clarify ideas.
5	Generating discussion	Solicits contributions from other members of the class.
6	Linking and applying	Points to relationships among mathematical ideas and mathematics and other areas of study/life.
7	Extending thinking	Extends the situation under discussion to other situations where similar ideas may be used.
8	Orienting and focusing	Helps students to focus on key elements or aspects of the situation in order to enable problem solving.
9	Establishing context	Talks about issues outside of mathematics in order to enable links to be made with mathematics.

Fig. 6.1. Types of questions used by teachers. (From Boaler and Brodie [2004, p. 776]).

As discussed in chapter 5, questions must be applied at appropriate moments during classroom interactions—moments that are defined by the goals of the lesson and students' progress in reaching those goals. Teachers who have carefully prepared by anticipating student responses to instructional tasks will be in a much better position to know when and how to use each of the question types.

Exploring questioning in Regina Quigley's classroom

The following excerpt (adapted with permission from the Institute for Learning, University of Pittsburgh) comes from Regina Quigley's fourth-grade classroom. The teacher and students have just begun a geometry unit in *Everyday Mathematics*. Before beginning the lesson depicted in the exchange that follows, the students had sorted polygons and non-polygons and identified the characteristics of polygons. They had also found the areas of rectangles and squares. Regina's goal for this lesson was for students to construct the formula for finding the area of a right triangle by manipulating premade cardboard right triangles against a backdrop of grid paper. She wanted students to realize that the areas of right triangles can be found either by embedding the triangle within a rectangle and then finding the area of the rectangle and dividing by 2, or by dividing one of the sides of the triangle by 2 and multiplying it by the other side of the triangle (the canonical formula for the area of a right triangle: $A = \frac{1}{2} bh$).

Regina has been working to develop a problem-solving culture that encourages students to formulate and discover solution paths and engage in discussions about the solution paths. The following discussion ensued after students had worked in small groups to find a formula or rule for finding the area of the triangles shown in figure 6.2. Students were given graph paper, rulers, scissors, and cardboard triangles to use in their work.

ACTIVE ENGAGEMENT 6.1

Read the excerpt from Regina Quigley's class. Using the three question types highlighted in figure 6.1, classify the teacher's questions that appear in the transcript.

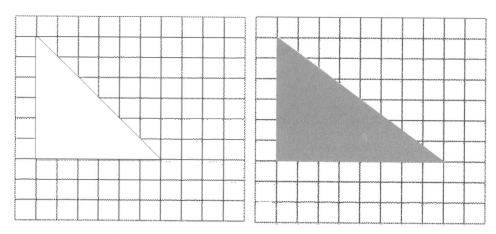

Fig. 6.2. Right triangles that Ms. Quigley gave her students

Ms. Quigley:	OK. I'm going to redirect you guys. I need your attention up here a little bit. And I'm looking at all these finds that you came up with and I heard all of you say these things. I need someone to share with me a rule or formula that they came up with to find the area of a triangle. Tammy.
Tammy:	[*Inaudible at first*] …When we got… We had two of them here. We had length times width divided by two.
Ms. Quigley:	[*Records on an overhead transparency (l × w) ÷ 2.)*] Where are you coming up with this?
Tammy:	Because when you cut the square in half, that's half, and, like, when you get, like, 36, 'cause that's a whole square, and half of it's 18, so, like, if you had another—any square—any square, and you did, um, the length times the width, and then you divided that in half, you'd get your answer.
Ms. Quigley:	How do you know to divide? Where are you getting this dividing by two? I'm curious about where you're coming up with that.
Tammy:	When we started with a whole square, it was 36. But then you have to cut it in half for a triangle.
Ms. Quigley:	Why do you… I'm wondering why you need to do that?

5

10

15

20	*Tammy:*	'Cause, it, um, so we could have a triangle. So we know how many halves. And in each one, we had 18 in each of our squares.
	Ms. Quigley:	OK, so you are saying that the triangle takes up one-half of the square and that since you could find the area of the square, you just took one-half of it to find the area of the triangle. Right?
25	*Tammy:*	Right.
	Ms. Quigley:	Is there another way that… Can someone tell me, or share with me, another way that we could write the same formula to see if it would still work? Quinn.
	Quinn:	Um, half times… um, half of length times width.
30	*Ms. Quigley:*	Is that the same thing?
	Quinn:	Yeah.
	Ms. Quigley:	[*Records* ½ $(l \times w)$.] David?
	David:	Yeah, because when you write 2, it's just another way of saying "half."
	Ms. Quigley:	Oh, when I say "two"… Anytime that I say "two," it's the same as saying "half"?
35	*David:*	No, when you say "length times width *divided by two.*"
	Ms. Quigley:	Oh, "*divided by two.*"
	David:	It's just like saying "multiplied by half."
40	*Ms. Quigley:*	What if I did this? I'll put it in red so you can see it. What if I did this? [*Writes* ½ $(l \times w)$ *next to* $(l \times w)/2$ *on the overhead transparency.*] Do those mean the same thing? I need some people who haven't participated to help me out. Do you think that those mean the same thing? Louis.
	Louis:	I think that you could come up with 18 with either one 'cause that's the same thing as the other one.
45	*Ms. Quigley:*	How do you know that?
	Louis:	I think it's the same because, um, half of length times width equals 18. Half of 36 is 18. I think it is the same because, um, it's just another way of saying "36 divided by 2."
	Ms. Quigley:	Does everyone agree with Louis? What about you, Jason?
50	*Jason:*	I agree with him that it's the same thing. We have one-half of length times width. It's just the opposite of the other thing. It just was length times width, and then we divided by 2.
55	*Ms. Quigley:*	OK. So we could represent the formula as either $(l \times w)/2$ or ½$(l \times w)$. I am going to move to the next problem. How can we represent the area of this triangle as a rule or formula? Angela? [*Draws a right triangle with a height of 6 and a base of 8 on grid paper at the overhead, as shown in gray in fig. 6.2.*]
	Angela:	You could make it a square and then take half of it: 48/2 = 24. The triangle is 24 squares.
60		[*Ms. Quigley motions Angela to the overhead, where she draws a 6 × 8 rectangle around the triangle; Ms. Quigley writes $(l \times w)/2$ next to Angela's drawing.*]
	Ms. Quigley:	OK. Can someone tell me another way to find the area of this triangle?
	Tanya:	You could cut the length in half and then take that times the width.

65 Ms. Quigley: So, now you're saying that I can do half of the length times width. I'm confused about where the parentheses go, or if I even need them. Can I write it like this? [*Writes ½ × l × w on the overhead.*]

Tanya: Yeah.

Ms. Quigley: How do you know I can do that?

70 Tanya: Because ½ of 8 is 4, and 4 times 6 is 24. That is the same number as we got before.

Ms. Quigley: So, can I *always* do this formula [*pointing to ½ × l × w*] and get the same answer as with the other two formulas that we've been using? How could we know for sure?

75 Tanya: Charlene and I cut the length in half. When we fit the small piece against the bigger triangle, we could make a rectangle…

Ms. Quigley: Can you come to the overhead and show us what you mean?

[*Tanya draws on a transparency and explains how she and Charlene rotated the "smaller piece" and placed it on the hypotenuse to form a rectangle that has a length that is half the length of the original 6 × 8 rectangle, as in fig. 6.3.*]

80 Tanya: So the area of this "new rectangle" will be 4 × 6, or 24.

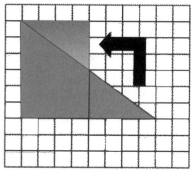

Fig. 6.3. Tanya's illustration of why ½ × l × w works

Ms. Quigley: Derrick, can you come up to the overhead, and using Tanya's diagram, repeat what Tanya just said that she and Charlene did?

Derrick: They broke the triangle into two pieces at the halfway mark along the base here. Then they took the broken-off piece and placed it, like a puzzle piece, up here to make a new rectangle. If you take the area of the new rectangle, it is 4 × 6, or 24.

Ms. Quigley: Thank you, Tanya, and thank you, Derrick. So Tanya has just shown us how taking ½ of the length, or what Derrick called the base, and multiplying it by the width can give us the exact same area as taking ½ of the length times the width of the bigger rectangle. Is there another way? James, we haven't heard from you today yet.

|James:| [*After a considerable pause*] You can cut the other side of the triangle in half and still get the same answer.|
|Ms. Quigley:| Can you show us how? [*Waits while James displays the arrangement shown in fig. 6.4.*] James, please tell us what you did.|

95

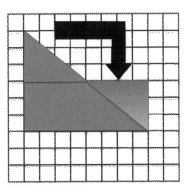

Fig. 6.4. James's illustration of why ½ × *w* × *l* works

|James:| Instead of cutting along the bottom, the 8, I cut the other side in half. That gave me 3. Then I turned this smaller triangle kind of upside down and put it in this corner. That made a new rectangle that was 8 × 3.|
|Ms. Quigley:| What is the difference between what James did and what Tanya did?|
|Vanessa:| Tanya took ½ of the bottom, and James took ½ of the side. Either way, it gave us the same answer.|
|Ms. Quigley:| Yes! If we want to call the bottom the "length," and the side the "width," [*points to the bottom and side, respectively, of the 6 × 8 triangle*], what Tanya and James have shown us is the equivalence of these two formulas [*writes ½ × l × w and ½ × w × l on the overhead transparency*]. And remember, earlier we found that ½ × *l* × *w* is also the same as (*l* × *w*)/2. All of these formulas are the same, and they all will work to give the area of a right triangle.|

100

105

Analyzing questioning in Regina Quigley's classroom

This excerpt provides examples of several of the question types shown in figure 6.1. Typically, teachers start to change their interaction style by "trying out" question type 5, *generating discussion*. We see Regina Quigley using questions of this type at several junctures. Her opening statement (lines 3–4), "I need someone to share with me a rule or formula that they came up with to find the area of a triangle," is a good example of how teachers can begin a whole-group discussion by soliciting ideas or solution strategies from students. A little later in the discussion (lines 26–28), Regina solicits additional contributions by asking, "Is there another way that… Can someone tell me or share with me another way that we could write the same formula to see if it would still work?" This, too, is a good way to open the floor for additional student contributions, especially alternative strategies. Generating discussion questions can also be used to try to solicit contributions from students who are not participating, as illustrated in lines 41–42, where Regina says that she needs to hear from students who haven't yet participated. A little later in the discussion, she uses generating discussion questions once again as she opens the floor for discussion about the second problem (the triangle with a height of 6 and a base of 8; lines 54–55) and seeks additional ways of finding the area of the triangle (line 62).

Generating discussion questions are important, but they must be used hand in hand with other types of questions to deepen the discussion. *Probing questions* (type 4 in fig. 6.1) can be used to help students to explain their thinking, as in lines 8–9 ("Where are you coming up with this $[(l \times w)/2]$") and line 15 ("How do you know to divide?"). Both of these questions pushed Tammy to articulate the reasoning behind her thinking, explaining that the triangle can be viewed as embedded inside a 6×6 square and as taking up half of the area of that square. Using her knowledge of how to compute the area of the square ($l \times w$), Tammy divided the resulting area (36) by 2 to compute what half of the area of the square would be, or the area of the triangle.

A little later, Regina uses a probing question again, in this case to ascertain if the student has a misconception and, if not, to get the student to represent his thinking more clearly. After David casually states, "When you write 2, it's just another way of saying 'half'" (line 33), Regina probes: "Oh, when I say 'two'… Anytime that I say 'two,' it's the same as saying 'half'?" This turns out to be very helpful, since David then clarifies that "divided by two" is same as multiplying by one-half.

Like generating discussion questions, most teachers also find probing questions easy to use and typically will get the hang of this style of questioning quickly. Students, too, quickly become accustomed to being asked the *whys* and *hows* of their thinking and will often proceed to provide them without being asked. However, teachers need to learn how to discern when this question type can be expected to pay dividends and when it cannot. Asking students to explain their thinking further makes sense only if the problem has some "grist," and a student's method of approaching it illuminates some underlying concepts or ideas, as was the case in Regina Quigley's classroom. The student's explanation that the triangle could be viewed as half of a square can be seen as shedding light on how students can use what they know in a novel way to solve for something that they don't know. Concepts of area, and of what it means to take one-half of something, also surfaced and became available for further discussion.

Probing questions don't have to ask for discursive explanations. Another moment in the excerpt when a probing question turned out to be exceedingly useful occurred when Ms. Quigley was publicly puzzling over whether $\frac{1}{2} \times l \times w$ would always produce the same answer as $\frac{1}{2} (l \times w)$. After Tanya noted that she and her partner Charlene had used scissors to cut the 6×8 triangle and then rotated the smaller piece, Regina probed their thinking by asking Tanya to display what they had done at the overhead projector (line 76). This public display of how the geometric and symbolic representations "matched" was an important step in cementing the idea that either of these two formulas would always work with right triangles.

The excerpt shows Regina Quigley using questions of type 3, *exploring mathematical meanings or relationships*, at two critical junctures. In the first case, Regina used type 3 questions to drive home the point that dividing by 2 is the same thing as multiplying by $\frac{1}{2}$ (lines 34; 39–41). The general mathematical principle at work here is that multiplying by a fraction is the same as dividing by its reciprocal ($a \times b/c = a \div c/b$).

In the second case, later in the excerpt, Regina used questions of type 3 to expose the idea that $\frac{1}{2} (l \times w)$ is the same as $\frac{1}{2} \times l \times w$ and the same as $\frac{1}{2} \times w \times l$. This experience highlights the commutative and associative properties of multiplication. For example, in lines 64–66, Regina asks if she can write $\frac{1}{2} (l \times w)$ as $\frac{1}{2} \times l \times w$ (asking, in other words, whether the grouping makes a difference). Although she did not choose to refer explicitly to the properties, the class was clearly establishing the equivalence of different ways of sequencing and grouping factors through their thinking and reasoning.

A bit later, Regina asks the question, "How could we know for sure?" That is, how could we know for sure that we would always get the same answer by using either $\frac{1}{2} (l \times w)$ or $\frac{1}{2} \times l \times w$ (lines 71–73). This question leads to Tanya's demonstration of how cutting and rotating the triangle leads to the exact same area as taking $\frac{1}{2}$ of the larger 6×8 triangle. The mathematical idea at play here is equivalence, shown symbolically by using the commutative and associative properties and geometrically through the diagrams.

Moves to Guide Discussion and Ensure Accountability

Many mathematics teachers believe that students learn through sharing their ideas, listening to and critiquing the ideas of others, and by having others critique their approaches to solving problems. Classroom discussions in which these activities occur do not materialize out of thin air. Rather, they are planned, through anticipating and monitoring; orchestrated, through selecting, sequencing, and connecting; and executed, through skillful use of identifiable discussion moves on the part of the teacher.

Almost all good classroom discussions begin in the same way: by inviting a student to share how he or she solved a particular problem. After the initial student response, however, classroom discussions diverge—separating into the relatively rare fruitful ones and the much more frequent unproductive show-and-tells. It turns out that issuing an invitation to students to reveal their thinking is a relatively easy thing to learn how to do. And most students will comply. We have witnessed many classroom discussions in which one student after another comes to the front of the room to explain how he or she solved a problem. Typically, however, teachers treat all presentations as equally good, they ask few questions of the students, and they do not connect different student presentations with one another or the disciplinary ideas under investigation.

Learning how to follow up on the ideas that surface in such student presentations is much more difficult. Attainment of this skill separates good teachers from fledgling teachers. In this book, we have provided concrete suggestions for orchestrating productive discussion that are rooted in the five practices. In addition to these practices, however, teachers need a *set of moves* that will help them lead whole-class discussions in which students share their thinking with one another in respectful and academically productive ways.

In this section, we identify particular moves that effective teachers use to position students advantageously both in relation to one another and in relation to the mathematics. Positioning in relation to other students includes feeling entitled and expected to question and comment on the ideas that others have presented and expecting that one's own ideas, questions, and understandings will be taken seriously. Positioning in relation to the mathematics includes feeling entitled and expected to raise questions and reach conclusions through reasoned inquiry regarding the concepts, principles, and methods of the discipline, in contrast to simply adopting what one is told, uncritically and superficially.

Although there are many moves that teachers can use to lead productive classroom discussions, we have chosen to focus on five in this book: (1) revoicing, (2) asking students to restate someone else's reasoning, (3) asking students to apply their own reasoning to someone else's reasoning, (4) prompting students for further participation, and (5) using wait time (Chapin, O'Connor, and Anderson 2003, pp. 12–16).

Revoicing

Especially in the early stages of getting discussions going in the classroom, student contributions are often difficult to hear and sometimes difficult to understand. Yet, all students need to have access to what a student has said if they are expected to think about and comment on it. For this reason, repeating part or all of a student's response is often a worthwhile move for teachers.

When repeating a student's contribution, it is important that the teacher guard against stripping authorship from the student. If the student stated the contribution too softly, the teacher should (after giving the student the opportunity to state it more loudly) simply repeat it so that everyone can hear it. If the idea was not well stated and thus was hard for other students in the class to grasp, the teacher should reformulate it to make it more comprehensible, but without changing the idea. If the meaning is at all in question, the teacher should also ask the student to respond to the revoiced contribution and verify whether or not it is correct.

We can find an example of revoicing in lines 22–24 of Regina's classroom discussion of finding the area of right triangles. After giving Tammy several chances to explain why she knew to divide the area of the square by 2 to get the area of the right triangle, Regina was not convinced that Tammy had stated the reason clearly enough for everyone in the class to have "gotten it." So she revoiced Tammy's contribution by saying, "So you are saying that the triangle takes up one-half of the square and that since you could find the area of the square, you just took one-half of it to find the area of the triangle." After restating her interpretation of what Tammy had said, she checked back with Tammy to assess its veracity by asking, "Right?"

Sometimes revoicing can be done effectively at the end of more than one student contribution. For example, during the sharing and summarizing phase of the Calling Plans task discussed in chapter 5, Nick Bannister wanted to ensure that students understood why plan A was cheaper in the long run than plan B. Several students offered partially coherent explanations; for example, Colin said, "So the one with the higher fee costs more if you only talk a little bit, but if you talk more, it eventually gets cheaper. Like the fee gets spread out over more minutes" (lines 378–81). Soon after, referring to her graph, Lynette said, "Well, you can see that plan A starts at 5 and goes up, and plan B starts at 2 and goes up. But B is steeper than A, so it goes up faster … because the cost per minute is more" (lines 382–85). Nick then summarized: "So Colin and Lynette are pointing out that although plan A costs more than plan B for zero minutes, since it costs less per minute than plan B, it will at some point cost less" (lines 385–87). This revoicing served to crystallize the main point that the cost-per-minute feature of the plans was the driving force in making plan A cheaper than plan B in the long run.

Asking students to restate someone else's reasoning

Instead of revoicing a student's idea themselves, teachers can ask another student to restate, in his or her own words, what the first student has just said. Again, the idea is not to interpret, evaluate, or critique the response. A student's restating of another student's contribution marks the contribution as being especially important and worth emphasizing. As such, it signals to the author that his or her ideas are being taken seriously, and it puts the rest of the students in the class on notice that they have a second chance to catch up on something really important—and that they had better be prepared, lest one of them be the next person asked to restate another student's contribution. A teacher should ask only one student to restate what another student has said if the ideas are clear and comprehensible.

An example of a student's restating what another student has said appears in lines 81–82 of Regina Quigley's classroom discussion. Tanya has just shown how $\frac{1}{2} \times l \times w$ makes sense geometrically, by cutting off and rotating a piece of a 6×8 rectangle. This was a key moment in the discussion because it tied the canonical formula for the area of a right triangle—$A = (\frac{1}{2})bh$—to a geometric representation that showed the rearrangement of two subareas of the triangle to form a 6×4 rectangle with the same area. By calling Derrick to the overhead projector to restate what Tanya had done, Regina reinforced the importance of Tanya's work, testing to see if other students had followed her reasoning, and giving everyone another opportunity to view the relationship between a geometric and a symbolic representation. By using language that was not identical to Tanya's, Derrick provided students with alternative access to her reasoning.

Asking students to apply their own reasoning to someone else's reasoning

An important part of productive classroom discussions is comparing one's own reasoning with that of others. Sometimes two students find that they agree with each other. At other times, their ways of reasoning may differ, but both are correct. This experience provides an opportunity to find out how two different pathways can lead to the same understanding or solution. Finally, students can find that their reasoning differs from that of other students and that they disagree on a fundamental idea or a solution to a problem, thus revealing the need to figure out whose reasoning is correct.

All of these scenarios offer opportunities for students to enhance their understanding of mathematics and how it works. The key is for teachers to prompt students to give more than their agreement or disagreement and to press them to explain why they agree of disagree.

In the Calling Plans lesson (chapter 5), one of Nick's goals was for students to make connections among different representations of the two calling plans. Near the end of the lesson, Nick knew that most students had correctly reasoned about the table representation and, similarly, that students who had generated the symbolic representation (the equations) also had reasoned correctly. He now wanted them to be able to "find" their reasoning inside the "space" of the other representation.

Nick asked Tony to explain how his group came up with the equation for each plan (lines 399–400). When Tony finished explaining how his group had used the cost per minute for each plan times the total number of minutes and added the monthly fee to create the equations, Nick asked the other groups—those students who had started with tables and had not made equations at all—what they thought about what Tony was saying. In essence, Nick was asking them to apply their reasoning about their tables to Tony's group's reasoning about their equations. This led into a nice discussion of where one would find the coefficient of m (.04 for plan A) and the constant monthly fee in the tables (lines 410–424).

Similarly, in line 49, Regina Quigley wants to make sure that everyone is on the same page with respect to the equivalence of ½ ($l \times w$) and ($l \times w$)/2. After Louis stated that the two expressions were the same and why, Regina asked: "Does everyone agree with Louis? What about you, Jason?" Jason proceeds to give his version of why the expressions are the same: "I agree with him that it's the same thing. We have one-half of length times width. It's just the opposite of the other thing. It just was length times width, and then we divided by 2." In this case, the students' reasoning aligned with each other's (and with that the previous two speakers, Quinn and David), but each student stated the case in a slightly different way. Because the equivalence of these two expressions was an important point to establish before moving on, having students apply their own reasoning to other students' reasoning was a way for Regina to catalyze the meaning-making that undergirds this idea and have it stated in different ways.

Prompting students for further participation

After some initial ideas are on the table, more students can be asked to join in. Prompting a wider range of students to weigh in adds more ideas to the discussion. The invitation for further participation can either be extended in an open-ended way near the moment of closure on an important point ("Does anyone have any other thoughts or comments on what we've been talking about?") or more strategically. For example, in chapter 5, we saw Nick Bannister trying to get the students to consider what the students who had sketched the graphs of the two calling plans might have used as the basis for their sketch. After discussing how the students knew to place points at (0, 2) and (0, 5), the conversation turned to the observation that the graphs were straight lines. When Nick prompted Mary to explain why she had stated that the graph was linear, he received a half-complete response: "They're going by the same amount, so that's why I'm thinking that it's linear" (lines 340–41). At this point, Nick opened it up to the class, saying, "OK. Does anyone want to add to that?" (line 342). This question led to a lively discussion among four students (James, Colin, Tamika, and Tony) regarding how each plan keeps going up by a constant amount (and never changes) and how one can find that constant rate of change in the tables, though it is not immediately evident in tables that increase by multiples of 10 instead of one minute at a time (see fig. 5.4). In this case, Nick's use of the question, "Does anyone want to add to that?" produced a much more detailed explanation of why the graphs would be linear than had Mary's initial response.

Using wait time

Giving students time to compose their responses signals the value of deliberative thinking, recognizes that deep thinking takes time, and creates a normative environment that respects and rewards both taking time to respond oneself and being patient as others take the time to formulate their thoughts. It all diversifies participation. Rather than the same three or four students dominating the discussion, more students are able and willing to join in if time is provided for them to create something that they feel comfortable about sharing.

Using wait time can be advantageous at several different junctures of a classroom discussion. Perhaps most familiar to teachers is the commonly heard refrain that teachers should wait at least 10 seconds for a student to raise a hand after asking a question. However, teachers should also provide wait time after calling on a particular student (Chapin, O'Connor, and Anderson 2003). For example, after Tanya presented a diagram that showed why $\frac{1}{2} \times l \times w$ would work as a formula to find the area of a right triangle, Regina Quigley asked if there might be another way to configure the area of a right triangle. She directed this question specifically to James, saying, "James, we haven't heard from you today yet" (line 91). Although James took his time in responding, Regina could tell that he was thinking—and she gave him the time that he needed. As shown in the next line of the transcript, James came up with a totally different and completely valid way of demonstrating how to find the area of the 6×8 triangle.

In chapter 5, near the beginning of part 4 of the vignette of the Calling Plans task, we see yet a third juncture at which wait time could be useful. After the class had established (through several lines of reasoning) that 51 minutes (and not 50 minutes) was the point at which plan A becomes less expensive than plan B, Nick asked if anyone had any questions and then paused for 10 seconds (lines 297–98). With no one responding, he decided to move on. This use of wait time served to give students an opportunity to digest an important finding and to raise any lingering questions that might occur to them. In addition, the pause marked closure to one phase of the discussion and the opening of another.

Conclusion

The skills discussed in this chapter complement and deepen instruction guided by the five practices. Their use will help teachers to unearth, probe, and stimulate student thinking. Because a rich supply of student thinking is the grist for effective use of the five practices, the skills discussed in this chapter are important forerunners of classroom instruction based on the five practices.

We have provided skills for stimulating student thinking in two main categories. First, we identified and illustrated ways in which teachers can interrogate individual students about their thinking to move it to deeper levels. Working at their best, questions that *probe* and *explore meaning and relationships* press students to explain the *why* of their thinking and, in so doing, help them discover the methods of mathematical reasoning as well as the relationships at the heart of the central ideas of the discipline. When mathematical methods of reasoning and important ideas come to the surface, the teacher benefits from having grist to work with in the discussion. The students benefit by realizing—perhaps for the first time in their lives—that they personally can reason about and make sense of mathematics.

We have also discussed a second category of skills for stimulating students' thinking. These skills are designed to make use of social interaction as a way of catalyzing complex thinking and reasoning. Many learning theorists contend that all complex thinking has its roots in social interaction (e.g., Vygotsky [1978]). Mathematical reasoning has certainly benefited from the back and forth of assertions and counter-assertions throughout history (Lakatos 1976). Inside the classroom, listening to, making sense of, and building on others' thinking are practices that teachers can develop through the set of moves that we have outlined in the second section of this chapter. These moves can bring student reasoning to the surface and invite others to both add to that reasoning and question it. Over time, norms are developed for how one should behave in a mathematics classroom—norms that can go a long way toward changing students' views of mathematics and of themselves as thinkers and problem solvers.

In the next chapter, we situate preparation for classroom discussions in a broader context of lesson planning, where teachers are asked to consider additional issues related to facilitating the learning of all students.

TRY THIS!

- If you made an audio or video recording as suggested in the "Try This!" at the end of chapter 5, transcribe 10 minutes of the discussion that you recorded.

- See if you can identify any of the question types discussed in the first half of chapter 6 (see the highlighted rows of the chart in fig. 6.1) or any of the five talk "moves" discussed in the second half of the chapter. For each question or move identified, consider what impact the question or move had on the subsequent discussion. (You might also want to consider where use of one the question types or one of the moves may have led to a more productive outcome.)

CHAPTER 7

Putting the Five Practices in a Broader Context of Lesson Planning

The primary focus of the book up to this point has been on considering the steps that can be taken before and during a lesson to ensure that the discussion that occurs at the end of the lesson is productive—that is, that the discussion accomplishes something that is important mathematically and that the mathematics to be learned by students is explicitly addressed. A productive discussion, we have argued, requires setting clear learning goals for the lesson and selecting a task that has the potential to meet these goals (chapter 2), engaging in the five practices of anticipating, monitoring, selecting, sequencing, and connecting (chapters 3, 4, and 5), and asking questions that promote non-algorithmic thinking and holding students accountable for actively engaging in public discourse (chapter 6).

In this chapter, we now broaden our focus to consider lesson planning more generally, considering how the five practices fit into a broader context of lesson preparation. We begin with a discussion of lesson planning that extends beyond anticipating—the first of the five practices—then we move on to a consideration of what Nick Bannister (the teacher whose practice we investigated in chapters 4 and 5) did in planning his lesson that might have previously been hidden from view, and we conclude with a summary of the aspects of planning that a teacher may want to record to support the actual enactment of the lesson and to serve as a record for future enactments.

ACTIVE ENGAGEMENT 7.1
- What do you do to plan a lesson (e.g., what questions do you think about, what sources do you consult, what do you write down)?

- To what extent does the cognitive demand of the task (see fig. 2.3) that you are using affect the level of planning in which you engage?

Lesson Planning

Good advance planning is the key to effective teaching. Good planning "shoulders much of the burden" of teaching by replacing "on-the-fly" decision making during a lesson with careful investigation into the *what* and *how* of instruction *before* the lesson is taught (Stigler and Hiebert 1999, p. 156). According to Fennema and Franke (1992, p. 156):

> During the planning phase, teachers make decisions that affect instruction dramatically. They decide what to teach, how they are going to teach, how to organize the classroom, what routines to use, and how to adapt instruction for individuals.

Lesson plans, however, have traditionally been seen as directions for executing particular lessons with an emphasis on procedures and structures, with limited attention to how the lesson will help students develop understanding of key disciplinary ideas. Such plans are often written to fulfill contractual obligations rather than to investigate deeply the *what* and *how* of instruction. Consider, for example, the lesson plan created by Paige Morris, shown in figure 7.1, in preparation for a lesson on systems of linear inequalities.

Periods 4 and 6:	**QUARTER PORTFOLIOS ARE DUE TODAY**
Objective	Graphing systems of linear inequalities
Warm-up	Review linear inequalities
Procedures	pp. 30–31
Homework	pp. 464–466
	(1, 2, 4, 6, 11, 13, 18)

Fig. 7.1. Paige Morris's lesson plan. (From Mossgrove [2006, p. 13].)

Paige's plan focuses on what she will *cover* during the lesson (pages 30–31 of the textbook) and what students will *do* (complete the warm-up and the assigned homework). This "Post-it note lesson plan" shoulders none of the burden of teaching, and hence all of the decisions that Paige makes during the lesson will be "on the fly," since she appears to have done little thinking in advance about the *what* and *how* of teaching. As Brahier (2000) noted, lesson effectiveness is related to the quality of lesson preparation. If we believe this to be the case, then we might expect that the lesson designed by Paige is ill fated before she even sets foot in the classroom.

Now consider a lesson plan created by Keith Nichols for a lesson that he was teaching on exponential functions, based on the Devil and Daniel Webster task, shown in figure 7.2. Keith's lesson plan, shown in figure 7.3, provides some evidence that he considered not only what task students would work on, but how he would set up the task and the questions that he might ask at the end of the lesson. He also appears to recognize that students might be confused about the distinction between the salary that the devil pays to Daniel at the beginning of the day and Daniel's net salary once he pays the devil his commission at the end of the day. Keith planned to address this confusion before students begin working on the problem (see the gray shading in fig. 7.3). Although much remains unspecified in Keith's plan (e.g., what are the key mathematical ideas that students are to learn? what solutions are students likely to produce during their exploration of the task? what difficulties might students encounter as they engage in the task? how will the key mathematical ideas be made salient?), he has investigated the lesson in more than a superficial way.

The Devil and Daniel Webster

The devil made a proposition to Daniel Webster. The devil proposed to pay Daniel for services in the following way:

On the first day, I will pay you $1000 early in the morning. At the end of the first day, you must pay me a commission of $100, so your net salary that day is $900. At the start of the second day, I will double your salary to $1800, but at the end of the second day, you must double the amount that you pay me to $200. Will you work for me for a month?

Fig. 7.2. The Devil and Daniel Webster task. (From Burke et al. 2001, pp. 27, 66–68; this task and a related lesson plan can also be found at http://illuminations.nctm.org.)

Algebra: The Devil and Daniel Webster

Goal: Consider a real-life problem that has an exponential context. Find an exponential formula that fits the situation. Pass back tests

Launch

 Ask: Can anyone think of a real-life situation that could be expressed with exponents?

 Ask: Does anyone know what a commission is?

     Hand out worksheets

     Read story

 Have students write their impression of whether or not they would take the offer. Make certain that students understand how the process works. The amount that they have left at the end of the day is the amount of their salary minus the commission. This difference is what gets doubled for the next day.

Explore

 Students work to complete the worksheet in small groups.

Summary

 Ask: What kind of relationship do the commission and number of days have? (exponential)

 Ask: What formula did you come up with to tell you the amount of commission, based on the number of days?

 Ask: What do you think the relationship between the number of days and the salary is?

 Ask: Do you think it is exponential?

 Ask: What would it be if we didn't have to worry about subtracting the commission?

 Refer to worksheet. Start with 1000. To get to the next day, you do "about" what to the 1000? (double it). Then to get to the next one after that you do about what to 2000? (double it).

 OK, but you're not really just doubling them. You have 1000, and you double it and then subtract a little. Then you double 2000 and subtract a little more. Then you double 4000 and subtract a little more than before.

 Ask: What do you think his graph would look like? (it would start going up and then slope downward)

 Ask: Does the graph for commission ever slope downward? (no)

 If commission is a bad thing for you and it is always increasing, and salary is a good thing for you and it only increases for a little while, then does this sound like the kind of permanent job you would want?

 Ask: What does it mean if the line representing salary crosses the *y*-axis? (it means that you are making negative $)

 Ask: Does this seem like a reasonable real-life situation? Why not?

 Demonstrate on a graphing calculator how to find the exponential regression formula. Recall how to do this for linear regression. If all of the data points are actually generated by an equation, then **ExpReg** will give you that equation.

 Try it for salary to see what you get. How accurate do you think this is? (Look at *r*-squared value.)

Fig. 7.3. Keith Morris's lesson plan. (From Mossgrove [2006, pp. 286–87].)

We could think about lesson planning as falling on a continuum from left to right, with *no planning* on the extreme left and *thoughtful and thorough planning* on the extreme right. From this perspective, we might place Paige Morris near the left side of the continuum and Keith Nichols somewhere to her right, as shown in figure 7.4. This raises a question that we will consider in the next section: What constitutes a thoughtful and thorough lesson plan—perhaps one that would be associated with the gray dot in figure 7.4—and what is the work that teachers must do to create such plans?

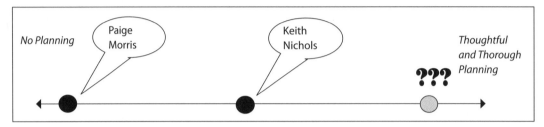

Fig. 7.4. The lesson-planning continuum

Developing thoughtful and thorough lesson plans

In recent years, lesson planning has received increased attention as a vehicle for improving teaching and learning. This is due, in part, to the success of Japanese lesson study (Lewis 2002; Stigler and Hiebert 1999). What is noteworthy about the planning in which teachers engage as part of the lesson study process is the attention that they pay to anticipating what students are likely to do during a lesson, generating questions that they themselves could ask to promote their students' thinking during the lesson, considering the kinds of guidance that they could give to students who show misconceptions in their thinking, and determining how to end the lesson in a way that will advance students' understanding. In this planning process, the attention shifts from the teacher as the key actor in the classroom to the students: What are they thinking? How are they making sense of the content? How can their mathematical understanding be advanced during the lesson?

Smith, Bill, and Hughes (2008) provide a framework for developing lessons that uses students' mathematical thinking as the critical ingredient in developing their understanding of key disciplinary ideas. The Thinking Through a Lesson Protocol (TTLP), shown in figure 7.5, is intended to promote the type of careful and detailed planning that is characteristic of Japanese lesson study. The purpose of the TTLP is to scaffold teachers' work in planning a lesson by providing a set of questions organized around three key activities: (1) selecting and setting up a mathematical task, (2) supporting students' exploration of the task, and (3) sharing and discussing the task. In the sections that follow, we discuss the relationship between the TTLP and the five practices, paying particular attention to the aspects of the TTLP that are not captured in the five practices.

ACTIVE ENGAGEMENT 7.2
- Review the TTLP shown in figure 7.5.

- How is the TTLP similar to or different from the lesson-planning process that you described in Active Engagement 7.1?

- Do you think that the differences between the TTLP and your current planning process matter? If so, in what ways?

PART 1: SELECTING AND SETTING UP A MATHEMATICAL TASK

What are your mathematical goals for the lesson (i.e., what do you want students to know and understand about mathematics as a result of this lesson)?

In what ways does the task build on students' previous knowledge, life experiences, and culture? What definitions, concepts, or ideas do students need to know to begin to work on the task? What questions will you ask to help students access their prior knowledge and relevant life and cultural experiences?

What are all the ways the task can be solved?

- Which of these methods do you think your students will use?
- What misconceptions might students have?
- What errors might students make?

What particular challenges might the task present to struggling students or students who are English Language Learners (ELL)? How will you address these challenges?

What are your expectations for students as they work on and complete this task?

- What resources or tools will students have to use in their work that will give them entry into, and help them reason through, the task?
- How will the students work—independently, in small groups, or in pairs—to explore this task? How long will they work individually or in small groups or pairs? Will students be partnered in a specific way? If so, in what way?
- How will students record and report their work?

How will you introduce students to the activity so as to provide access to *all* students while maintaining the cognitive demands of the task? How will you ensure that students understand the context of the problem? What will you hear that lets you know students understand what the task is asking them to do?

PART 2: SUPPORTING STUDENTS' EXPLORATION OF THE TASK

As students work independently or in small groups, what questions will you ask to—

- help a group get started or make progress on the task?
- focus students' thinking on the key mathematical ideas in the task?

- assess students' understanding of key mathematical ideas, problem-solving strategies, or the representations?
- advance students' understanding of the mathematical ideas?
- encourage *all* students to share their thinking with others or to assess their understanding of their peers' ideas?

How will you ensure that students remain engaged in the task?

- What assistance will you give or what questions will you ask a student (or group) who becomes quickly frustrated and requests more direction and guidance in solving the task?
- What will you do if a student (or group) finishes the task almost immediately? How will you extend the task so as to provide additional challenge?
- What will you do if a student (or group) focuses on non-mathematical aspects of the activity (e.g., spends most of his or her (or their) time making a poster of their work)?

PART 3: SHARING AND DISCUSSING THE TASK

How will you orchestrate the class discussion so that you accomplish your mathematical goals?

- Which solution paths do you want to have shared during the class discussion? In what order will the solutions be presented? Why?
- In what ways will the order in which solutions are presented help develop students' understanding of the mathematical ideas that are the focus of your lesson?
- What specific questions will you ask so that students will—

1. make sense of the mathematical ideas that you want them to learn?
2. expand on, debate, and question the solutions being shared?
3. make connections among the different strategies that are presented?
4. look for patterns?
5. begin to form generalizations?

How will you ensure that, over time, *each* student has the opportunity to share his or her thinking and reasoning with their peers?

What will you see or hear that lets you know that *all* students in the class understand the mathematical ideas that you intended for them to learn?

What will you do tomorrow that will build on this lesson?

Fig. 7.5. The Thinking Through a Lesson Protocol (TTLP). (From Smith, Bill, and Hughes [2008, p. 134].)

Relationship between the TTLP and the five practices

In figure 7.5, we have provided annotations to indicate the ways in which the five practices are embedded within the TTLP. Although there is clearly more to the TTLP than the five practices, they are in fact a significant subset of the work of planning. We have argued that before teachers can begin to enact the five practices, they must first set a goal for the lesson and select a task. As the annotation suggests, this is also a critical step in the more general lesson-planning process.

Also prominent in the TTLP is anticipating. This includes both anticipating the ways in which a student might solve a task (both correctly and incorrectly), as shown in part 1 of the TTLP, and the questions that teachers might develop that would prepare them to respond to the things that students do as they work on the task (the first set of bullets in part 2 of the TTLP). In part 3 of the TTLP, we see explicit attention to selecting, sequencing, and connecting (as shown in the annotations in figure 7.5), and this work is a large part of what the teacher must do in preparing for a productive discussion.

One thing that may be noticeable by its absence in the TTLP is any connection to monitoring. Monitoring is a process that happens *during* instruction, and while it is facilitated by carefully anticipating prior to the lesson, little additional planning can support this activity other than the creation of a monitoring sheet such as that created by Nick Bannister (see fig. 4.3). The completed monitoring sheet (such as the one shown in fig. 5.3), can serve as a record of which students have had the opportunity to share their thinking and reasoning with their peers (one of the questions in part 3 of the TTLP).

Beyond the five practices

Although the five practices (along with "practice 0"—determining the goal of the lesson) capture much of what is involved in the planning process, we argue that each question in the TTLP deserves some consideration as a teacher prepares for a lesson. The chart in figure 7.6 lists each of the questions in the TTLP that is not addressed in the five practices and provides a rationale for considering the question during the planning process. Although a teacher might be able to respond on the spot, without prior thought, to some of the issues that are addressed in the TTLP questions (shown in the first column of the chart) (e.g., an English language learner [ELL] is confused about the wording of the task; a group finishes the task quickly and is left with nothing to do; students ask for calculators, which are locked in a cabinet), it would be difficult to attend to all these issues "online" without any prior attention to them and still keep the lesson moving in a productive direction.

Questions from TTLP that are not addressed by the five practices	Rationale for considering the question during the planning process
What particular challenges might the task present to struggling students or to students who are English Language Learners (ELL)? How will you address these challenges?	Meeting the needs of all learners is critical. Students for whom English is not a first language or students who struggle in mathematics may need more support than other students. Hence, teachers must carefully consider factors such as the groups into which they place students, the resources that they provide to support students' entry into the task, and the attention that they pay to vocabulary and context (e.g., do students understand what a calling plan is?). Teachers' attention to this level of detail will help ensure that all students have access to the content of the lesson.
What are your expectations for students as they work on and complete the task?	Students need to know what they will be expected to produce as a result of their work on the task and the resources that they will have with which to produce it. This knowledge will allow students to begin their work with a clear sense of purpose and direction. To this end, the teacher must determine what the products of the lesson will be and have the materials available for students to produce them.
How will you introduce students to the activity so as to provide access to *all* students while maintaining the cognitive demand of the task?	The cognitive demand of a task can be lowered if the teacher provides too much information when the task is first introduced. Alternatively, providing too little information can result in students not understanding what the problem is asking. Therefore, it is important for the teacher to consider how to strike a balance between providing sufficient guidance for students to enter the task but not so much that all the challenge has been removed.
How will you ensure that students remain engaged in the task?	For students to learn what the teacher intended and to participate actively in a discussion, they must first engage with the task. Some students have trouble getting started and become easily frustrated. If the teacher is not prepared to get them back on track quickly, they may choose to disengage completely. This result, in turn, often gives rise to off-task behaviors that can be both unproductive and disruptive. Alternatively, some students work at a much faster pace and finish a task quickly. The teacher needs to be prepared to address the needs of students on either end of this continuum by preparing additional scaffolding to assist struggling students and extensions to challenge more advanced students.
What will you see or hear that lets you know that *all* students in the class understand the mathematical ideas that you intended for them to learn?	Teachers must consider how they will know whether students have learned what they had intended. Doing so could involve developing questions that will provide insight into students' thinking, designing homework that will give students time to think about a set of ideas independently, creating an end-of-class reflection or exit slip that asks students to consider some aspect of the lesson, or developing a more formal means of assessing learning. It is important for the teacher not to equate completion of a task with understanding of the underlying ideas.
What will you do tomorrow that will build on this lesson?	It is important to consider how one lesson fits with the next to ensure that instruction is coherent and cohesive. Developing an understanding of a particular mathematical idea does not take place within one 45-minute period but rather extends over a series of lessons. Teachers need to consider how knowledge builds over time and how prior knowledge is solidified, broadened, and deepened in subsequent lessons.

Fig. 7.6. A chart showing questions from the TTLP and the rationales for considering them

In our discussion in chapter 4 of Nick Bannister's planning, we did not explicitly discuss any of the questions that appear in the chart in figure 7.6. That is not to say that Nick did not consider any of these issues—only that we chose not to make them focal in our highlighting of his attention to the five practices. It is hard to imagine that he didn't consider some of these issues, given that his lesson went so smoothly. For example, Nick clearly had set expectations for how students would work on the task, thus addressing the second question in column 1 in the chart in figure 7.6. He had determined that students would work in groups (see the list of groups in fig. 4.4) and that they would make posters that they would share (lines 74–77). It also appears that Nick made the necessary supplies available (e.g., chart paper, markers, rulers, as well as graphing calculators). Students seemed to know what to do and had the resources with which to do it.

Nick also seems to have considered the last two questions listed in the chart in figure 7.6. By assigning homework that asked students to explore one of the key ideas that he wanted them to learn (i.e., two functions "switch positions" at the point of intersection, so that the one that was on "top" before the point of intersection is on the "bottom" after it), he could assess the current state of students' understanding. In addition, the homework could easily serve as a way to launch the subsequent lesson and to press the students more directly about why intersecting functions "switch positions" before and after the point of intersection, and whether two linear functions will always have a point of intersection. Although the specific homework assignment was generated during class by a question raised by Latasha (i.e., will the plan with the cheaper cost per minute always be less expensive, no matter what the fee is?), it was closely connected to what Nick had planned to assign (lines 394–98).

Our point here is that a teacher who thinks through the questions on the TTLP prior to a lesson will be prepared to deal with much of what happens during the lesson. Although the lesson plan—the physical artifact—represents the outcome of the thinking process and serves as a historical record of the lesson, it is the *level of thinking* that goes into the preparation of the plan that matters most. A teacher with whom we have worked said this quite simply: "You have to study the lesson in and out. How you're going to orchestrate it. Otherwise it could be a flop."

Creating a permanent record of the lesson

Although it is the thinking that goes into the preparation of a lesson that is important, creating some record of the decisions about the lesson is critical for two reasons. First, the written plan serves as a reminder of key decisions so that teachers don't have to keep all of the details in their heads. It supports the teachers as they enact the lesson, reminding them of the course of action that they have set. Second, the written plan serves as a record of the lesson that teachers can store for future use, revise, and share with colleagues. The lesson plan, along with the monitoring sheet that is completed during the lesson, provides a good picture of the intent and some insight into the outcome of the lesson.

Let's consider the usefulness of several different lesson plans. The lesson plan created by Paige, discussed earlier in the chapter, provides limited support for teaching the lesson. Even if Paige engaged in thinking deeply about the lesson, it is unlikely that what she chose to write down would provide her with any support during the lesson or any record of what she would want to do in the future. As it turned out, Paige was not prepared to deal with many things that occurred during the lesson, including not realizing that the answer key in the back of the students' textbook was not correct, because she had not taken the time to solve for herself the problems that she had assigned (Mossgrove 2006).

Although Keith's lesson plan was more elaborate than Paige's and included pointers for setting up the task and questions that he might ask students during the lesson, he was not clear about what he thought students would do or what he wanted the outcome of the lesson to be. As a result, the lesson was about completing the task—not about understanding the mathematics embedded in it.

If a lesson plan provides both support during the lesson and a historical record for teachers to consult for future enactments of the lesson, what might the plan look like? Smith and Cartier (2009) devised the Lesson Plan Template, which is based on the TTLP but targets four key areas: task, instructional support, learning goals, and evidence. This Lesson Plan Template was used in creating the lesson plan shown in figure 7.7 for the Calling Plans task.

Instructional Support

What tools or resources will students have to use in their work that will give them entry to, and help them reason through, the activity?

- Students will work in their preassigned groups of 4.
- Each student will get a copy of the task.
- Each group will have a sheet of poster paper.
- Students will have access to graphing calculators, rules, colored pencils, and markers as needed.

*What questions might you ask students that will support their exploration of the activity and **bridge** between **what they did** and **what you want them to learn** (boxes joined by arrow)?*

To be clear on what students actually did, begin by asking a set of questions such as, How did you get that? What does this mean? Does that make sense? Once you have a clearer sense of what the student understands, move on to the appropriate set of questions below.

Correct Approaches

- How did your table help you find the answer to the question?
- What do you think the graphs will look like? Why do you think that?
- What does (50, 7) represent in this problem? Why is it important? Will any two lines intersect? How do you know?
- Where would you find the cost per minute in the table, graph, and equation?
- Where would you find the monthly fee in the table, graph, and equation?
- Why do companies A and B "switch positions" after the POI? What is going on here? Can you make a general statement about this?

Possible Difficulties

1. How would you write five dollars and four cents using dollar and cent notation? How does this compare to what you have now?
2. What would it mean to talk zero minutes? How much would it cost?
3. Draw students' attention to the rows in the table where the two plans changed position relative to each other. What is happening here? Can you predict what the graph of the two equations would look like? Can you explain why this is happening?
4. What do 4 and 5 represent in the problem? Which one changes as you talk more, and which one doesn't? What would it cost for 10 minutes by using your equation? Does this make sense?

Task

What is the main activity that students will be working on in this lesson?

Long distance company A charges a base rate of $5.00 per month plus 4 cents a minute that you're on the phone. Long distance company B charges a base rate of only $2.00 per month but charges 10 cents per minute used. How much time per month would you have to talk on the phone before subscribing to company A would save you money?

What are the various ways that students might complete the activity?

Correct Approaches

- Make a table with increments of 10 minutes and determine the point of intersection (POI) by finding the entry with the same cost for the same number of minutes
- Make a table with increments of 20 minutes; then make a graph to find the POI
- Write an equation and use to points to create a graph and then find POI
SHARE AT LEAST ONE TABLE, GRAPH, AND EQUATION

Possible Difficulties

1. Confuse .04 with .4 and 4
2. Not include zero minutes in the table
3. Not sure what to do if the POI doesn't show up in the table
4. Confuse cost per minute and monthly fee

Learning Goals (Residue)

What understandings will students take away from this activity?

1. recognize that there is a point of intersection between two unique, non-parallel linear equations that represents where the two functions have the same x- and y-values;

2. understand that the two functions "switch positions" at the point of intersection because the function with the smaller rate of change will ultimately be the function closer to the x-axis; and

3. make connections between tables, graphs, equations, and context by identifying the slope and y-intercept in each representational form.

Evidence

What will students say, do, produce, etc. that will provide evidence of their understandings?

- Students will create posters that show how they determine when company A was cheaper, using tables, graphs, equations, and context to explain what they did and why it works.

- Students will create different calling plans for homework. This will provide evidence of whether they understand how the monthly fee and the cost per minute influence the graph of the functions and help in determining which one will be cheaper in the long run.

Fig. 7.7. A lesson plan for the Calling Plans task that uses the Lesson Plan Template created by Smith and Cartier (2009)

"Task" (the left box in the figure) refers to what the students will work on, the approaches that they might use to solve the task, and the difficulties that they might encounter along the way. "Learning Goals" (the upper right box in fig. 7.7) refers to what students will know as a result of engaging with the task. The arrow that connects the task and learning goals is intended to imply the connection between the two: the point of the task is to provide students with an opportunity to learn the mathematics as specified in the learning goals. "Instructional Support" (the middle box in fig. 7.7) is the bridge between the tasks and learning goals and refers to both the resources that will support students' work on the task and the questions that the teacher will ask to make connections to the mathematical ideas and to help students make progress on the task. "Evidence" (the box on the lower right in fig. 7.7) refers to the indicators that will let the teacher know what students understand. The placement of evidence underneath the "Learning Goals" box is not arbitrary. It calls attention to the requirement that evidence must be related to the goals for learning.

The lesson plan shown in figure 7.7 is not intended to capture all the thinking that a teacher did in preparation for a lesson on the Calling Plans task. Rather, it is intended to serve as a record of key decisions made in advance of the lesson as the teacher thought through the questions on the TTLP. It is a record that the teacher can refer to, if needed, during the lesson and can archive following the lesson. A lesson plan such as this can help the teacher keep an eye on the lesson goals and specific ways to support students in achieving them.

We now want to return to the question posed earlier: What constitutes a thoughtful and thorough lesson plan? We consider the lesson plan in figure 7.7 to be one version of such a plan, and we propose it as a candidate for the position indicated by the gray dot on the continuum in figure 7.4. Unlike the other plans that we have considered, it shoulders much of the burden of teaching by focusing on what students are to learn (goals), what they will do (tasks), and how the teacher will meet them where they are and take them where they need to go (instructional support). Although the TTLP provides a critical set of questions to consider as a teacher plans for instruction, the Lesson Plan Template (shown in fig. 7.7 in connection with the Calling Plans task) highlights a subset of the questions raised in the TTLP that can help a teacher navigate the lesson and accompanying discussion as they unfold.

Conclusion

Our intent in this chapter—and in this book more generally—is to argue the importance of planning for instruction in advance of a lesson. Although the five practices provide teachers with a mechanism for improving the quality of the mathematical discussions that take place in their classrooms, these practices will be most effective when teachers consider them within a broader set of questions about teaching and learning.

Planning is a "premier teaching skill" (Stigler and Hiebert 1999, p. 156)—one that has a significant impact on the quality of students' instructional experiences in the classroom. It is a skill that can be learned and greatly enhanced through collaborations with colleagues. It is likely that Keith Nichols and Paige Morris would have benefited tremendously from planning their lessons with more experienced colleagues. As beginning teachers, they had relatively few experiences on which to draw in preparing their lessons and would have benefited from the wisdom of experience provided by veteran teachers. In the next chapter, we will discuss the kinds of support needed by teachers to become skillful planners and implementers of instruction.

TRY THIS!

- Use the TTLP to plan a lesson. Record key aspects of your planning using the Lesson Plan Template.
- Teach the lesson.
- Reflect on the impact of the TTLP and related Lesson Plan Template on your ability to enact the lesson.

Working in the School Environment to Improve Classroom Discussions

G ood teaching does not develop in isolation. Although teachers usually orchestrate discussions in the privacy of their own classrooms, teachers' continued learning and motivation depend on the immediate environment in which they find themselves: their school and their professional learning communities. Although teachers often feel that they have limited impact on these environments, this does not have to be the case. This chapter discusses ways in which teachers can interact with colleagues and school leaders to secure the time, materials, and access to expertise that they need to learn and sustain the effort required to orchestrate productive discussions.

We begin this final chapter with the Case of Maria Lancaster. Maria, an early-career teacher, wanted to engage her students in more challenging mathematical work in a school environment where such work was not the norm and did not appear to be valued. Through conversations with colleagues, and ultimately the principal, she was able to find the support that she needed to take a risk and try to change the status quo. We conclude the chapter with a discussion of the steps that teachers can take to form communities within their schools that can provide support for instructional improvement efforts.

Looking for Support: The Case of Maria Lancaster

Maria had the good fortune of attending a teacher education program where she had the opportunity to learn about the importance of anchoring instruction in mathematical learning goals and student thinking. By the time that she had completed her course work and student-teaching experience, Maria was convinced that students learn what
5   they have the opportunity to learn. If students are given the opportunity to grapple with complex tasks, to observe good models of thinking and reasoning, and to justify their solutions, they will develop a view of mathematics as meaningful and as something that they personally can engage with and understand. By contrast, if students spend their time "solving" problems by rote use of taught procedures, they will come to view math-
10   ematics as sterile, uninteresting, and making sense only to the "geeks."

Beginning her first job was a different story. Although Maria was thrilled to be hired in a prestigious school district with a reputation for progressive education, she quickly learned that the middle school mathematics department was focused on teaching

15 students procedures with limited, if any, attention to concepts and understanding. Students rarely had the opportunity to learn how to think and reason their way through non-routine problems. In her first year, Maria kept her head low and used the district-mandated textbook—and supplemented it as much as possible with more cognitively rich projects and tasks.

20 A discussion at the end of her first year of teaching with her grade-level colleague, Mark, made Maria realize that the frustrations that she had experienced were not hers alone. Together, Maria and Mark decided to start an after-school reading group—open to any interested teacher—which would focus on how to manage instruction using high-level, cognitively demanding tasks. Both Mark and Maria had been struggling with the question of how to "get to" the "point" of

25 their lessons when their students often took wildly divergent approaches to tasks. Moreover, comments made by the principal following his observations of their classes suggested that he was concerned that their students, although seemingly engaged, were not learning the "nuts and bolts" of mathematics. Maria and Mark were worried about their students' learning, as well.

30 The following September, Mark and Maria were joined by one other teacher, Clare, and the three of them selected their first reading—the article "Orchestrating Discussions" (Smith et al. 2009). They selected this article because it seemed to tackle the problems that they all were experiencing head-on. Getting students to talk was easy; assuring that classroom talk was productive, yet respect-

35 ful of the ideas that students brought to the table, was extremely difficult. Mark said that he felt as though he was always jumping in and correcting students. Both Maria and Clare were worried about letting students go on in unfruitful directions for too long. The article provided a set of practices (the five practices discussed in this book) that the authors claimed would help to take some of the improvisa-

40 tion out of teaching. That is, the practices would help teachers to anticipate what might happen and to plan ahead for how to deal with specific ways that students might approach the problem.

Reading about the five practices was one thing; enacting them, all three teachers were sure, would be another. In particular, they all felt daunted by the

45 article's recommendation to plan lessons so thoroughly. So they decided to start small by implementing the Bag of Marbles task featured in the article (see fig. 8.1). The article had already identified the possible solution strategies that students might use, so the first step—anticipating—was already done! After they had studied the various solution strategies, Maria started to feel more comfort-

50 able with the lesson material and offered to teach the lesson and to try to enact the other practices: monitoring, selecting, sequencing, and connecting. With the help of the principal, Mark and Clare were released from other duties so that they could observe Maria teaching the lesson. The principal too decided to participate in the observation.

Ms. Rhee's math class was studying statistics. She brought in three bags containing red and blue marbles. The three bags were labeled as shown below:

Bag x	Bag y	Bag z
75 Red 25 blue	40 Red 20 blue	100 Red 25 blue
Total = 100	Total = 60	Total = 125

Ms. Rhee shook each bag. She asked the class, "If you close your eyes, reach into a bag, and remove 1 marble, which bag would give you the best chance of picking a blue marble?"

Which bag would you choose? _____

Explain why this bag gives you the best chance of picking a blue marble. You may use the diagrams above in your explanation.

Created by the QUASAR assessment team, under the direction of Suzanne Lane at the University of Pittsburgh; appeared on the QCAI (QUASAR Cognitive Assessment Instrument) at grades 6-7-8.

Fig. 8.1. The Bag of Marbles task. (From Smith et al. [2009].)

55   During the observation, Mark and Clare used the tool that appeared in the article to monitor students' work (see fig. 8.2). They spent a lot of time closely observing students as they worked in groups, sometimes asking them questions. The principal, by contrast, stayed at the back of the room during the entire lesson.

Strategy	Who and What	Order
Fraction Determine the fraction of each bag that has blue marbles (x is ¼; y is $1/3$; z is $1/5$). Decide which of the three fractions is largest ($1/3$). Select the bag with the largest fraction of blue marbles (bag y).		
Percent Determine the fraction of each bag that has blue marbles (x is $25/100$; y is $20/60$; z is $25/125$). Change each fraction to a percent (x is 25%; y is 33 $1/3$%; z is 20%). Select the bag with the largest percent of blue marbles (bag y).		
Ratio (Unit Rate) Determine the part-to-part ratio that compares red to blue marbles for each bag (x is 3:1; y is 2:1; z is 4:1). Determine which bag has the fewest red marbles for every 1 blue marble (bag y).		
Ratio (Scaling Up) Scale up each bag so that the number of blue marbles in each bag is the same (e.g., x is 300 R and 100 B; y is 200 R and 100 B; z is 400 R and 100 B). Select the bag that has the fewest red marbles for 100 blue marbles (bag y).		
Additive Determine the difference between the number of red and blue marbles in each bag (x is 50; y is 20; z is 75). Select the bag that has smallest difference (bag y).		
Other		

Fig. 8.2. Tool for monitoring students' work on the Bag of Marbles task. (From Smith et al. [2009].)

60   Afterwards, Maria felt pretty good about the lesson, but she was still worried about what the others would think, especially the principal. She was beginning to put her finger on what she needed to work on: listening deeply to what
students were saying so that she could understand how they were thinking about
the problem and then build on this thinking as she helped them to explore the
mathematics at the heart of the lesson. Doing so, she realized, took a great deal of
65   concentration and focus.

At the end of the day, the four of them met briefly to discuss the lesson. The
monitoring sheets that Mark, Claire, and Maria had each used during the lesson—to collect data regarding what students were doing and thinking—grounded
their discussion. Mark, Clare, and Maria discussed the similarities and differences
70   in their observations and interpretations of the strategies that various students
were using. This was exceedingly helpful to Maria because both Mark and Clare
were able to make sense of some students' strategies in ways that had eluded her.
The next time that she taught this task, she thought to herself, she would be better
at recognizing these subtle variations on the anticipated strategies that appeared in
75   the article.

For example, Maria was not sure about the solution presented by Kalib (see
fig. 8.3). Although he selected the correct bag, his approach didn't exactly match
the identified strategies. Mark and Clare helped Maria see that Kalib had used
a fraction strategy but focused on the fraction of a bag that was *red marbles*. The
80   bag with the smallest such fraction would have the largest fraction of blue marbles.

Bag x is ¾ red. Bag y is ⅔ red. Bag z is ⅘ red.
Because ⅔ is the smallest fraction, bag y has the smallest fraction of red marbles. So, bag y must have the largest fraction of blue marbles. Best chance of picking a blue marble with bag y.

Fig. 8.3. Kalib's solution to the Bag of Marbles task

Mark and Clare also discussed their thoughts about which strategies they would
have shared, in what order, and why. Here, too, their perspectives were eye-open-
ing. Although Maria had prepared for this lesson more thoroughly than for most,
she still had to think on her feet—the clock kept ticking! Having access to two
85   extra sets of perceptions—from colleagues unencumbered by having to teach—
was revealing all sorts of new possibilities for Maria regarding how she might have
used and supported her students' thinking more productively.

The principal, who had not used the tool, began to realize that he had a completely different perspective on the lesson than did Mark and Clare—and that he
90   had less to offer to help Maria improve. Without the monitoring tool to guide
him toward particular solution paths and prompt him to examine student work
and listen to student thinking, the principal had viewed the lesson as somewhat
incoherent, with everyone doing his or her own thing. Listening to the three
teachers converse, he realized that another layer of teaching and learning was go-
95   ing on to which he had no access.

Analysis of the Case of Maria Lancaster

Maria Lancaster is representative of many teachers who believe that they are alone in their desire to build their teaching on supporting their students as they engage in tasks that challenge them to think and reason. The turning point for Maria came during her end-of-the-year conversation with Mark (lines 19–29), who shared many of her concerns and desires for improving teaching. As Maria began her second year of teaching, her collaboration with Mark and Clare gave Maria the confidence and determination that she needed to begin to enact lessons in her classroom that required more of her students.

The co-observation in which Mark, Clare, Maria, and the principal engaged provided a critical shared experience for talking about teaching and learning. First, through the discussion, Maria came to see and understand things differently (e.g., the thinking behind solutions, such as Kalib's, which was not immediately clear to her—lines 76–80), and to gain more insight into ways that she needed to support her students. Second, her colleagues gave her alternative suggestions regarding ways that the discussion could have been orchestrated, highlighting how the selection and sequencing of different solutions can lead to very different outcomes. Finally, the observation and subsequent debriefing provided a valuable opportunity for the principal to reconsider the nature of the observations that he himself conducted and whether the surface features of what occurs in the classroom tell the whole story of what students are learning.

The three teachers—Maria, Clare, and Mark—formed a small but cohesive community that was focused on improving the quality of discussions in their classrooms. They were committed to working collaboratively and made the time after school to do so. Together, they were able to garner support from the principal, who provided release time so that Mark and Clare could observe Maria's class. As a result, the three teachers were positioned to move forward, and perhaps, over time, other teachers in the building would join them in their efforts at instructional improvement.

In the remainder of the chapter, we discuss how teachers can overcome some of the obstacles that appear to be standing between them and the type of teacher they want to be and how teachers can begin to work in collaboration with their colleagues and the principal.

Overcoming Obstacles

Perhaps the most debilitating obstacle that a teacher faces is the fear that his or her supervisor may not understand or support the approach to teaching advocated in this book. Without access to the deeper structure of learning that occurs in classrooms, principals often judge the "top layer" of activity as undisciplined or even chaotic. Not all principals will be as open-minded as Maria's principal appears to be. (And even Maria's principal may need more convincing that this approach to teaching will yield the test scores that his school needs to produce.) However, teachers like Maria, Mark, and Clare, who let their principal in on the fact that there is a powerful underlying logic to their approach, are taking an important first step. Moreover, the fact that this logic is grounded in theory and research on how students learn can help to convince skeptical principals that this approach to instruction is evidence-based.

The final "proof," of course, is student achievement. By using this approach, teachers help students develop the understanding that should put them in a good position to perform well on grade-level accountability tests. Studies of student performance in classrooms that use student-centered, standards-based curricula have demonstrated that students in these classrooms do as well on tests of basic skills as students taught with conventional, teacher-led curricula; on tests of conceptual understanding and reasoning, students taught with standards-based curricula do better than conventionally taught students (Chappell 2003; Putnam 2003; Swafford 2003). And, of course, teaching for understanding in a student-centered way compares favorably with the typical test prep approach, in which teachers give students practice on items that "look the same" as tested items, with little or no effort to develop students' understanding.

More work remains to be done, however, even after the fear of poor evaluations from a principal has been allayed. Chances are that teachers who are working to improve their instruction by using the five practices will be much harder on themselves than others will be. Once teachers start to see their practice "from the inside"—that is, from the perspective of student thinking—a much wider landscape of challenges and possibilities opens up to them. Yes, there are more misconceptions to be corrected than a teacher might have ever imagined, but there are also exciting glimpses of what might be possible, given the curiosity, creativity, and flexibility of the human mind. Teachers begin to see that their students' minds are active and that how they themselves manage their students' thinking plays into what students will learn.

For all of these reasons, teachers who find the five practices useful often work continually to improve. The first time that a teacher uses a particular instructional task, he or she may focus on anticipating and monitoring to learn more about how his or her students tend to respond to the task and what mathematical ideas can be brought forth from students' responses. The second time around, the teacher can use the information from the first enactment to make judicious choices about which approaches to be sure to select for class discussion. In later lessons, the teacher can use the information gathered in the previous lessons to begin developing effective methods of sequencing and connecting. Thus, over time, a teacher's facilitation of a discussion related to a particular task can improve, with progress accelerating if he or she works with other teachers, makes use of resources from research and curriculum materials, and consistently builds on records of what he or she has observed and learned during each effort.

Working with Others

Once teachers have seen the benefits of student-centered instruction—and have found the five practices to be a useful tool for managing discussions— they inevitably want to share their discovery with others. How can a teacher go from a small group of like-minded colleagues—in Maria's case, just three teachers—to a larger community of teachers who help students to learn in this way? In the following paragraphs, we explore several different approaches that teachers might consider in building a community of teachers who have a shared view of teaching and learning.

First, teachers can invite their colleagues to observe a lesson in which the five practices are being used. Rather than give the observers a "five practices road map" right off the bat, the demonstration teacher can enlist them to help by paying attention to which students are "getting it" and which aren't. In this way, the observers' focus will be on the students; once the share-and-summarize discussion begins, the observers should have some notions of the variety of student responses. Chances are good that they will then be positioned to notice what the demonstration teacher is able to "do with" these various understandings. If the teachers have indeed noticed the demonstration teacher's moves, the language of the five practices can then be attached to them.

A second approach would be for teachers to campaign for the principal to set aside common planning time for groups of teachers and to hire an outside consultant to help the group co-plan a lesson that one of them would then teach while the others observed. Common planning time is most productive when teachers have a specific task to perform and they are held accountable for that task. At the end of the semester, each co-planning group could be asked to present one demonstration lesson for the grade level or for the entire school. This is similar to a lesson study model, which has been shown to lead to an increased focus on student learning (Perry and Lewis 2010).

A third approach to broaden the community of teachers who are working together toward a common goal would be to work with the principal to design a process of curriculum selection that calls attention to the levels of cognitive demand in most of the tasks. As noted earlier, orchestrating productive classroom discussions is nearly impossible with low-level, procedurally based tasks. If teachers start out with a storehouse of good tasks, they will be much better positioned to begin work on the five practices. Indeed, if they faithfully follow a high-demand curriculum, they will quickly experience the *need* for the five practices. We have found it useful to use the Task Analysis Guide (discussed in chapter 2 and shown in fig. 2.3) to examine one common topic across all the textbooks under consideration.

A fourth approach would be to build a constituency and a demand for student-centered practice by starting a dialogue with educational stakeholders in the community. For example, a teacher might ask to speak at an education committee meeting of the school board to talk about exciting trends in mathematics teaching and learning. We have posted a PowerPoint presentation that could serve as a starting point for such a session. (For the presentation and other materials to support a discussion on cognitively challenging tasks, go to www.teacherscollegepress.com, select "Free Downloads" from the menu on the right, and scroll to "Implementing Standards-Based Mathematics Instruction" (Stein et al. 2009). Adding video clips that display local examples of student-centered practice would make the presentation even more powerful. The same PowerPoint presentation could be used with parents at open house nights or with the school board. An e-seminar, "Effective Mathematics Instruction: The Role of Mathematical Tasks (K–12)," available from the National Council of Teachers of Mathematics (go to http://www.nctm.org/profdev and select "E-Seminars"), might also be useful in introducing ideas related to the benefits of using cognitively challenging tasks in the classroom.

A final approach would be for teachers to convince their principals to attend a Lenses on Learning seminar, followed by professional development on the five practices, with the goal of encouraging principals to use a tool based on the five practices when they observe classes. (For information on Lenses on Learning seminars, go to www.mathleadership.org, and select Lenses on Learning (LOL) from the menu on the left side of the homepage.)

Conclusion

Maria Lancaster and teachers like her need not feel powerless to bring about change in their school environments. Through conversations with colleagues, a teacher may initially find one or two like-minded colleagues who together can begin to make changes in the way that mathematics is taught and learned, and these changes can serve as a catalyst for broader school-based reforms.

The work that we are proposing in this book—thoughtfully and thoroughly planning instruction around cognitively challenging tasks culminating in a whole-group discussion that makes the mathematics to be learned salient to students—is not easy. Although some teachers have taken on this challenge alone, working with colleagues can greatly enhance a teacher's effort. Teachers such as Maria, Mark, and Clare are committed to improving learning opportunities for their students, willing to examine current practices critically, and determined to make gradual improvements in practice. Hence, they are on a trajectory to be what Stigler and Hiebert (1999, p. 179) refer to as "star teachers of the twenty-first century." That is, they will be teachers "who work together to infuse the best ideas into standard practice. They will be teachers who collaborate to build a system that has the goal of improving students' learning in the 'average' classroom, who work to gradually improve standard classroom practices."

All teachers have the capacity to be stars—they just need access to opportunities to learn, reflect, and grow. This book provides such an opportunity. Working through the book alone or with colleagues, teachers can begin to make changes in their instructional practices that will improve the effectiveness of their teaching and the learning of students in their charge.

REFERENCES

Achieve. *Foundations for Success: Mathematics Expectations for the Middle Grades.* Washington, D.C.: Achieve, 2002.

Ball, D. L. "With an Eye on the Mathematical Horizon: Dilemmas of Teaching Elementary School Mathematics." *The Elementary School Journal* 93, no. 4 (1993): 373–97.

Bill, V. L., and I. Jamar. "Disciplinary Literacy in the Mathematics Classroom." In *Content Matters: A Disciplinary Literacy Approach to Improving Student Learning*, edited by S. M. McConachie and A. R. Petrosky, pp. 63–85. San Francisco: Jossey-Bass, 2010.

Bennett, J. M., E. B. Burger, D. J. Chard, A. L. Jackson, P. A. Kennedy, F. L. Renfro, J. K. Scheer, and B. K. Waits. *Mathematics Course 2.* Austin, Tex.: Holt, Rinehart, and Winston, 2007.

Boaler, J., and K. Brodie. "The Importance of Depth and Breadth in the Analysis of Teaching: A Framework for Analyzing Teacher Questions." In *Proceedings of the 26th Meeting of the North America Chapter of the International Group for the Psychology of Mathematics Education*, Toronto, Ontario, 2004.

Brahier, D. J. *Teaching Secondary and Middle School Mathematics.* Allyn and Bacon, 2000.

Bransford, J. D., A. L. Brown, and R. R. Cocking, eds. *How People Learn: Brain, Mind, Experience, and School.* Washington, D.C.: National Academy Press, 2000.

Burke, M., D. Erickson, J. W. Lott, and M. Obert. *Navigating through Algebra in Grades 9–12. Principles and Standards for School Mathematics* Navigations Series. Reston, Va.: National Council of Teachers of Mathematics, 2001.

Chapin, S. H., C. O'Connor, and N. C. Anderson. *Classroom Discussions: Using Math Talk to Help Students Learn, Grades 1–6.* Sausalito, Calif.: Math Solutions, 2003.

Chappell, M. "Keeping Mathematics Front and Center: Reacting to Middle-Grades Curriculum Projects Research." In *Standards-Based School Mathematics Curricula: What Are They? What Do Students Learn?* edited by S. L. Senk and D. R. Thompson, pp. 285–96. Mahwah, N.J.: Lawrence Erlbaum Associates, 2003.

Cuevas, C., and K. Yeatts. *Navigating through Algebra in Grades 3–5. Principles and Standards for School Mathematics* Navigations Series. Reston, Va.: National Council of Teachers of Mathematics, 2001.

Dewey, J. *The Child and the Curriculum.* Chicago: University of Chicago Press, 1902.

Doyle, W. "Work in Mathematics Classes: The Context of Students' Thinking during Instruction." *Educational Psychologist* 23 (February 1988): 167–80.

Engle, R. A., and F. C. Conant. "Guiding Principles for Fostering Productive Disciplinary Engagement: Explaining an Emergent Argument in a Community of Learners Classroom." *Cognition and Instruction* 20, no. 4 (2002): 399–483.

Fennema, E., and M. L. Franke. "Teachers' Knowledge and Its Impact." In *Handbook of Research on Mathematics Teaching and Learning*, edited by D. Grouws, pp. 147–64. Reston, Va.: National Council of Teachers of Mathematics, 1992.

Hantano, G., and K. Inagaki. "Sharing Cognition through Collaborative Comprehension Activity." In *Perspectives on Socially Shared Cognition*, edited by L. B. Resnick, J. M. Levine, and S. D. Teasley, pp. 331–480. Washington, D.C.: American Psychological Association, 1991.

Hart, K. *Children's Understanding of Mathematics.* London: John Murray, 1981.

Heller, P. M., A. Ahlgren, T. Post, M. Behr, and R. Lesh. "Proportional Reasoning: The Effect of Two Context Variables, Rate Type, and Problem Setting." *Journal of Research in Science Teaching* 26 (March 1989): 205–20.

Hiebert, J., A. K. Morris, D. Berk, and A. Jansen. "Preparing Teachers to Learn from Teaching." *Journal of Teacher Education* 58 (February 2007): 47–61.

Kaput, J., and M. M. West. "Missing-Value Proportional Problems: Factors Affecting Informal Reasoning Patterns." In *The Development of Multiplicative Reasoning in the Learning of Mathematics*, edited by G. Harel and J. Confrey, pp. 235–87. Albany, N.Y.: State University of New York Press, 1994.

Lakatos, I. *Proofs and Refutations: The Logic of Mathematical Discovery.* Cambridge: Cambridge University Press, 1976.

Lampert, M. *Teaching Problems and the Problems of Teaching.* New Haven, Conn.: Yale University Press, 2001.

Lappan, G., J. T. Fey, W. W. Fitzgerald, S. N. Friel, and E. D. Philips. *Connected Mathematics: Looking for Pythagoras.* Boston: Pearson Education, 2010.

Larson, R., L. Boswell, and L. Stiff. *Geometry.* McDougal Littel, 2004.

Lave, J., and E. Wenger, *Situated Learning: Legitimate Peripheral Participation.* N.Y.: Cambridge University Press, 1991.

Lewis, C. C. *Lesson Study: A Handbook of Teacher-Led Instructional Change.* Philadelphia: Research for Better Schools, 2002.

Mehan, H. *Learning Lessons: Social Organization in the Classroom.* Cambridge, Mass.: Harvard University Press, 1979.

Mossgrove, J. *Examining the Nature of Instructional Practices of Secondary Mathematics Preservice Teachers.* PhD diss., University of Pittsburgh, 2006. UMI Dissertation Services 3250964.

Perry, R., and C. Lewis. "Building Demand for Research through Lesson Study." In *Research and Practice in Education: Building Alliances, Bridging the Divide,* edited by C. E. Coburn and M. K. Stein, pp. 131–46. Lanham, Md.: Rowman and Littlefield, 2010.

Putnam, R. "Commentary on Four Elementary Mathematics Curricula." In *Standards-Based School Mathematics Curricula: What Are They? What Do Students Learn?* edited by S. L. Senk and D. R. Thompson, pp. 161–78. Mahwah, N.J.: Lawrence Erlbaum Associates, 2003.

Resnick, L. *Education and Learning to Think.* Washington, D.C.: National Academy Press, 1987.

Smith, M. S., V. Bill, and E. K. Hughes. "Thinking through a Lesson Protocol: A Key for Successfully Implementing High-Level Tasks." *Mathematics Teaching in the Middle School* 14 (October 2008): 132–38.

Smith, M. S., and J. Cartier. "The Lesson Plan Template." Created under the auspices of the Collaborative, Technology-Enhanced Lesson Planning as an Organizational Routine for Continuous, School-Wide Instructional Improvement Project, directed by M. K. Stein and J. Russell at the University of Pittsburgh, 2009.

Smith, M. S., A. F. Hillen, and C. Catania. "Using Pattern Tasks to Develop Mathematical Understandings and Set Classroom Norms." *Mathematics Teaching in the Middle School* 13 (August 2007): 38–44.

Smith, M. S., E. K. Hughes, R. A. Engle, and M. K. Stein. "Orchestrating Discussions." *Mathematics Teaching in the Middle School* 14 (May 2009): 548–56.

Smith, M. S., and M. K. Stein. "Selecting and Creating Mathematical Tasks: From Research to Practice." *Mathematics Teaching in the Middle School* 3 (February 1998): 344–50.

Stein, M. K., R. A. Engle, M. S. Smith, and E. K. Hughes. "Orchestrating Productive Mathematical Discussions: Helping Teachers Learn to Better Incorporate Student Thinking." *Mathematical Thinking and Learning* 10, no. 4 (2008): 313–40.

Stein, M. K., B. Grover, and M. Henningsen. "Building Student Capacity for Mathematical Thinking and Reasoning: An Analysis of Mathematical Tasks Used in Reform Classrooms." *American Educational Research Journal* 33 (Summer 1996): 455–88.

Stein, M. K., S. Lane, and E. Silver. "Classrooms in Which Students Successfully Acquire Mathematical Proficiency: What Are the Critical Features of Teachers' Instructional Practice?" Paper presented at the annual meeting of the American Educational Research Association, New York, April 1996.

Stein, M. K., M. S. Smith, M. A. Henningsen, and E. A. Silver. *Implementing Standards-Based Mathematics Instruction: A Casebook for Professional Development.* 2nd ed. New York: Teachers College Press, 2009.

Stigler, J. W., and J. Hiebert. *The Teaching Gap: Best Ideas from the World's Teachers for Improving Education in the Classroom.* New York: The Free Press, 1999.

Swafford, J. "Reaction to High School Curriculum Projects." In *Standards-Based School Mathematics Curricula: What Are They? What Do Students Learn?* edited by S. L. Senk and D. R. Thompson, pp. 457–68. Mahwah, N.J.: Lawrence Erlbaum Associates, 2003.

Van de Walle, J. A. *Elementary and Middle School Mathematics: Teaching Developmentally.* 4th ed. Boston: Allyn and Bacon, 2004.

Van de Walle, J. A., K. S. Karp, and J. M. Bay-Williams. *Elementary and Middle School Mathematics: Teaching Developmentally.* 7th ed. Boston: Pearson Education, 2010.

Vygotsky, L. S. *Mind in Society: The Development of Higher Psychological Processes.* Cambridge, Mass.: Harvard University Press, 1978.

5 Practices

Professional Development Guide

The purpose of this guide is to spark conversations about the key ideas in this book. Individual teachers reading the book may find the additional questions and suggestions thought-provoking, but the real benefit of this material is in supporting facilitated discussions in groups of preservice or practicing teachers.

Suggestions for Using the Activities in the Book

Throughout the book, two types of activities are embedded in the chapters for the purpose of engaging teachers: "Active Engagement" and "Try This!" Although each of these activities can be beneficial to an individual teacher working alone, they can stimulate interesting discussions in a group of teachers brought together for a common purpose.

ACTIVE ENGAGEMENT

Throughout the book, these activities offer suggestions to the reader about how to engage with a specific artifact of classroom practice that a chapter presents (narrative cases of classroom instruction, transcripts of classroom interactions, instructional tasks, samples of student work). These suggestions could be explored by a group of teachers and discussed in small- or large-group formats to identify different perspectives or solutions prior to reading the authors' analysis.

For example, in chapter 2, readers are invited to solve the Tiling a Patio task (see Active Engagement 2.4). A facilitator might invite teachers to work on this task in small groups, share different solutions, and then orchestrate a discussion of the task by using the five practices. This would provide teachers with access to different solution methods (several of which they will subsequently encounter in the Case of Darcy Dunn) and an opportunity to participate in the type of carefully orchestrated discussion that we are suggesting that they facilitate in their own classrooms.

In chapter 3, readers are asked to analyze the Case of Darcy Dunn and to identify instances where Darcy appears to be using the five practices (see Active Engagement 3.1). Here a facilitator might ask teachers to read the Case of Darcy Dunn in preparation for a whole-group discussion among teachers about the ways in which the five practices were or were not evident in Darcy's teaching practice. The discussion would provide an opportunity to get multiple ideas on the table and for teachers to provide justification for selecting specific events as instances of the five practices. Following a whole-group discussion, teachers could go on to read the analysis provided by the authors and to consider the extent to which they do or do not agree with the authors' perspective. This too could provide fodder for additional whole-group discussion. At the conclusion of this activity, teachers would have a clearer sense of what the five practices might look like in action and be better positioned for their work on the remaining chapters.

TRY THIS!

At the end of chapters 4, 5, 6, and 7, readers are invited to try out in their own classrooms the key ideas discussed in the chapter. At the conclusion of these chapters, the facilitator might suggest that teachers engage in the assignment, individually or collaboratively, and return to a subsequent session prepared to talk about their experiences.

For example, in the Try This! at the end of chapter 4, teachers are asked to select a high-level task and to engage in the first practice—anticipating. A facilitator might pair up teachers who teach the same content and ask them to begin to plan a lesson collaboratively, anticipating what students might do when presented with the task and how they will respond when they do it. Teachers could subsequently be put in groups of four, with each pair given the opportunity to share the task that they have selected and the solutions that they have anticipated. They could then receive feedback from their colleagues that they could use to revise the task or their expectations about what students will do. The Case Story Protocol (Hughes, Smith, Hogel, and Boston 2009) or the Noticing and Wondering Protocol (Smith 2009) could be used to facilitate respectful sharing and the production of useful feedback:

Hughes, E. K., M. S. Smith, M. Hogel, and M. D. Boston. "Case Stories: Supporting Teacher Reflection and Collaboration on the Implementation of Cognitively Challenging Mathematical Tasks." In *Inquiry into Mathematics Teacher Education,* edited by F. Arbaugh and P. M. Taylor, pp. 71–84, Monograph Series, vol. 5. San Diego, Calif.: Association of Mathematics Teacher Educators, 2009.

Smith, M. S. "Talking about Teaching: A Strategy for Engaging Teachers in Conversations about Their Practice." In *Empowering the Mentor of the Preservice Mathematics Teacher,* edited by G. Zimmermann, pp. 39–40; *Empowering the Mentor of the Beginning Mathematics Teacher,* edited by G. Zimmermann, pp. 33–34; and *Empowering the Mentor of the Experienced Mathematics Teacher,* edited by G. Zimmermann, pp. 35–36. Reston, Va.: National Council of Teachers of Mathematics, 2009.

Suggestions for Digging Deeper

Although many ideas presented in the book could be explored in more depth (e.g., questioning, accountable talk, lesson study), one idea that may require more attention is the cognitive demand of a mathematical task. This idea is discussed in chapter 2, but depending on the background and experiences of teachers, additional work may be needed in preparation for subsequent chapters, since this concept is fundamental to work on the five practices.

For example, a facilitator might engage teachers in a discussion of one of the following articles where related ideas are presented:

Smith, M. S., and M. K. Stein. "Selecting and Creating Mathematical Tasks: From Research to Practice." *Mathematics Teaching in the Middle School* 3 (February 1998): 344–50.

Stein, M. K., and M. S. Smith. "Mathematical Tasks as a Framework for Reflection: From Research to Practice." *Mathematics Teaching in the Middle School* 3 (January 1998): 268–75.

Or a facilitator might engage teachers in sorting a set of tasks with different levels of demand to assist them in developing sets of characteristics of tasks at each level. A set of tasks that could be used toward this end can be found in the following:

Smith, M. S., M. K. Stein, F. Arbaugh, C. A. Brown, and J. Mossgrove. "Characterizing the Cognitive Demands of Mathematical Tasks: A Sorting Activity." In *Professional Development Guidebook for Perspectives on the Teaching of Mathematics: Companion to the Sixty-sixth Yearbook,* pp. 45–72. Reston, Va.: National Council of Teachers of Mathematics, 2004.

Suggestions for Questions to Pose to Participants

The questions that follow are intended to engage teachers in further consideration of the ideas presented in the book and to elicit their beliefs and practices related to teaching and learning. The professional development facilitator can choose questions for participants to consider before reading the chapters or use them for post-reading discussion or reflection.

Introduction

1. Do you think discussions are an important feature of mathematics classrooms? Why or why not?

2. What experiences have you had in orchestrating discussions? What challenges have you encountered in your efforts to engage students in talking about mathematics?

3. Do you agree that students learn when they are encouraged to become authors of their own ideas and when their thinking is held accountable to key ideas in the discipline? Why or why not? What implications does this point of view have for teaching?

4. In the Leaves and Caterpillars vignette, David Crane allowed students to "author their own ideas," but he did not appear to hold students accountable for learning particular mathematical ideas. The authors suggested that to do so, he first needed to be clearer about what he wanted his students to learn.

   a. What might be an appropriate learning goal for a lesson that features the Leaves and Caterpillars task?

   b. How might the discussion have unfolded differently in Mr. Crane's classroom with this goal in place?

Chapter 1: Introducing the Five Practices

1. Telling would appear to be a more efficient means of communicating to students what they need to know. What are the costs and benefits of learning through discussion of student-generated solutions versus learning from carefully constructed teacher explanations?

2. How do you currently plan a lesson? To what extent do you focus on what you will do versus what students will do and think?

3. Anticipating is an activity that is likely to increase the amount of time spent in planning a lesson. What would you expect to be the payoff for this investment of time?

4. How might a monitoring chart such as the one shown in figure 1.1 be useful to you in your work?

5. Many teachers believe that questions arise "in the moment," as a result of classroom interactions. To what extent can teachers plan questions in advance of the lesson? What benefit might there be in having some questions ready prior to a lesson?

6. How might carefully selecting and sequencing students' responses affect the quality of the discussion? How would these practices give you more control over the discussion?

7. Why is connecting important? What is the teacher's role in helping students make connections?

Chapter 2: Laying the Groundwork: Setting Goals and Selecting Tasks

1. How would you describe the relationship between the goal for a lesson and the instructional activities in which students are to engage during the lesson?

2. How do you think the specificity of a goal can help you during a lesson?

3. The authors argue that what students learn depends on the nature of the task in which they engage. Do you agree with this point of view? Why or why not?

4. What do you see as the costs and benefits of using high-level (i.e., cognitively challenging tasks) as the basis for instruction?

Chapter 3: Investigating the Five Practices in Action

1. Do you think Darcy Dunn's lesson was effective? What leads you to that conclusion? What did she do beyond the five practices that may have contributed to (or detracted from) the quality of the lesson?

2. What, if anything, would you have liked to see Darcy Dunn do differently? How do you think the changes that you propose would have affected student learning?

3. Compare the instruction in Darcy Dunn's class with the instruction in David Crane's class. How were they the same, and how were they different? What impact do you think the differences may have had on students' opportunities to learn?

Chapter 4: Getting Started: Anticipating Students' Responses and Monitoring Their Work

1. What do you see as the advantages of solving the task in which students will engage? Is this something you routinely do? Why or why not?

2. Why might you want to anticipate both correct and incorrect approaches to solving a task?

3. How might a monitoring chart such as the one shown in figure 4.3 be useful to you in your work? (The same question was posed in connection with chapter 1. Has your view of the usefulness of this tool changed since you initially considered the value of the monitoring chart?)

4. Nick Bannister must have spent considerable time planning and thinking about this lesson. Under what circumstances might such an investment of time be worthwhile?

5. What, if anything, do you think Nick Bannister could or should have done differently in planning (part 1) and supporting students' work on the task (part 2)? Why would you make these changes?

Chapter 5: Determining the Direction of the Discussion: Selecting, Sequencing, and Connecting Students' Responses

1. Have you ever asked students in your classes to volunteer solutions to the task that they were assigned? What are the best and worst experiences that you have had when you used this strategy for sharing? How do you see selecting as leading to a more consistent outcome?

2. Under what circumstances or conditions do think it makes sense to publicly share incorrect approaches with students? How would you do this so that students were not left thinking that incorrect approaches were valid?

3. Does who presents a solution to a task really matter as long as the desired solutions are made public? Why or why not?

4. What, if anything, do you think Nick Bannister could or should have done differently in selecting and sequencing student responses (part 3) and in making connections among responses and with the mathematical ideas that were central to the lesson (part 4)? Why would you make these changes? What impact would you expect these changes to have on students' opportunities to learn?

Chapter 6: Ensuring Active Thinking and Participation: Asking Good Questions and Holding Students Accountable

1. To what extent to do you use the IRE pattern of questioning in your own classroom? What do you see as the advantages and disadvantages of this pattern of interaction?

2. How might the categories of question types identified by Boaler and Brodie be useful to you in expanding your repertoire of question types? What do you see as the potential value of such an enterprise?

3. Return to part 4 of the Case of Nick Bannister featured in chapter 5. Can you find examples of different question types in this segment of the lesson? What role did the different question types serve in supporting students' learning from and engagement in the lesson?

4. To what extent do you currently use the five talk moves in your instruction? What benefits do you see in incorporating some or all of these moves into your practice?

5. What, if anything, do you think Regina Quigley could or should have done to give her students better support in learning from and engaging in the lesson? Why would you make these changes? What impact would you expect these changes to have on students' opportunities to learn?

Chapter 7: Putting the Five Practices in a Broader Context of Lesson Planning

1. The discussion questions for chapter 1 asked you to describe how you planned a lesson. How does the process that you described compare with what is suggested in the TTLP? What do you see as the value, if any, of the breadth of questions that the TTLP asks you to consider?

2. How can a lesson plan "shoulder the burden of teaching"?

3. Under what circumstances can you imagine engaging in the level of planning suggested? What advantages can you see in doing so for a subset of lessons that might be particularly pivotal in learning specific concepts?

4. How might you mobilize your colleagues or your department to engage in collaborative lesson design? What might be the benefits of such work?

Chapter 8: Working in the School Environment to Improve Classroom Discussions

1. In your school environment, are you currently facing challenges that have an impact on the teaching and learning of mathematics in your classroom? If so, what are these challenges? How might you begin to address them?

2. Are cognitively challenging mathematical tasks a common feature of mathematics instruction in your school? If not, how might you take an active role in changing the status quo?

3. To what extent is your principal looking for practices compatible with the five practices when he or she observes your class? If your principal is focusing on a different set of practices, what are your options?

4. What lesson from Maria Lancaster's experience can you take that you can apply to your own situation?